E. *(handwritten)*

W9-CPC-713

Fun-to-Learn Bible Lessons: Grades 4 & Up

Group®
Loveland, Colorado

Fun-to-Learn Bible Lessons: Grades 4 and Up
Copyright © 1995 Group Publishing, Inc.

All rights reserved. No part of this book may be reproduced in any manner what-soever without prior written permission from the publisher, except where noted on handouts and in the case of brief quotations embodied in critical articles and reviews. For information, write Permissions, Group Publishing, Inc., Dept. BK, Box 481, Loveland, CO 80539.

Credits
Contributing Authors: Jody Brolsma, Lisa Lauffer, Liz Shockey, Cindy Smith, and
    Kathy J. Smith.
Book Acquisitions Editor: Mike Nappa
Editors: Jane Vogel and Michael Warden
Senior Editor/Creative Products Director: Joani Schultz
Copy Editor: Ann Carr
Art Director: Helen Lannis
Cover Art Director: Liz Howe
Designer: Janet Barker
Computer Graphic Artist: Joyce Douglas
Cover Photographer: Robert Cerri, The Stock Market
Illustrator: Shelley Dieterichs
Production Manager: Gingar Kunkel

Unless otherwise noted, Scriptures quoted from The Youth Bible, New Century Version, copyright © 1991 by Word Publishing, Dallas, Texas 75039. Used by permission.

Library of Congress Cataloging-in-Publication Data
Fun-to-learn Bible lessons. Grades 4 and up / (contributing authors, Jody
  Brolsma et al.).
    p. cm.
  ISBN 1-55945-604-3
  1. Bible—Children's use. 2. Bible—Study and teaching (Elementary) 3. Activity
programs in Christian education.
  I. Brolsma, Jody.
  BS618.F86   1995
  372.84—dc20   94-49160
                                                                       CIP

10 9 8 7 6   04 03 02 01 00 99
Printed in the United States of America.

Visit our Web site: www.grouppublishing.com

Contents

Introduction

Welcome to a resource filled with exciting, active Bible lessons for upper-elementary kids. These are fun together-times that will grab your kids' attention and teach powerful lessons from Scripture.

In *Fun-to-Learn Bible Lessons: Grades 4 & Up,* Sunday school teachers, vacation Bible school teachers, midweek directors, and anyone who has a heart for working with upper-elementary children will discover 20 simple-to-follow lessons that give students an overview of the entire Bible. The lessons combine lively learning, active participation, small group discussion, projects, and prayer to make the learning experience memorable for everyone.

As kids focus on a selection of 20 Old and New Testament passages, they'll experience exciting ways to apply the Bible to their lives. Together, you'll wind your way through topics such as

- creation,
- sin,
- hope in Jesus,
- the power of Jesus' resurrection,
- love,
- heaven,

and much more!

THE FUN-TO-LEARN LESSONS

Each lesson in *Fun-to-Learn Bible Lessons: Grades 4 & Up* contains at least six exciting activities. Activities are fast-paced because children have short attention spans. The following elements are included in each lesson:

- **Introduction**—One or two paragraphs that provide an overview of the lesson's topic.
- **A Powerful Point**—A concise statement of the lesson's objective, telling what the children will learn.
- **A Look at the Lesson**—An outline including activity titles and estimated completion times. These times may vary according to your class size.
- **The Fun-to-Learn Lesson**—Exciting, quick, Scripture-based activities. Kids experience each lesson through active learning using all five senses.

Lessons include interesting projects, interactive discussion, creative prayers, active object lessons, learning games, and much more. All necessary handouts are included. They're easy to use, and you have permission to photocopy them for local church use.

Enjoy *Fun-to-Learn Bible Lessons: Grades 4 & Up.* Mix and match these Bible lessons for any gathering of upper-elementary children and watch your kids grow in their understanding of the Bible, in confidence, in friendships, and in faith!

1. What a Wonderful World (Creation)

The creation story is a wonderful picture of God's innovation, wisdom, power, and most of all, his love for us. Sometimes we forget that *we* are as much a part of creation as the trees, flowers, mountains, and animals around us. In fact, we're a very special part.

Children don't often miss the wonder of the world around them. But it's important that while we point out the amazing things God has created, we don't ignore the most amazing creation of all—us! In this lesson, students will discover that they are an important, vital part of God's creation.

A POWERFUL POINT

We are a special part of God's wonderful world.

A LOOK AT THE LESSON

1. Ashley Is an Acorn (6 minutes)
2. Creation and Chaos (8 minutes)
3. Made Just for You (7 minutes)
4. Bubble Gum Creations (8 minutes)
5. Pass It On (8 minutes)
6. Way to Go, God! (8 minutes)
7. Thanks, God (6 minutes)

THE FUN-TO-LEARN LESSON

1. Ashley Is an Acorn

Form a circle. Say: **To start today,** think of something God made that starts with the first letter of your name. You're going to be acting out your words, so choose something that has good actions. For instance, Ryan may want to choose a rattlesnake instead of a rock! Keep your chosen word a secret until it's your turn to act it out. Let's start with the person whose name is closest to the end of the alphabet.

Have kids act out their chosen objects while the rest of the class guesses. After everyone has had a turn, ask:

● **What other descriptive words come to your mind when you think about this world God created?**

● **What do those words tell you about God?**

● **What's it like for you to know that God made you?**

Say: **We are a special part of God's wonderful world. Let's look at some of the awesome things God has made.**

2. Creation and Chaos

(You'll need newsprint, colored markers, and Bibles.)

Tape an 8-foot-long section of newsprint to the wall and give kids colored markers. (If newsprint isn't available, use a chalkboard and give kids colored chalk.)

Form pairs and assign each pair one of the passages below. (If you have fewer than 20 students, give each pair more than one passage. If you have more than 20 students, use some of the passages more than once.)

- Genesis 1:1-2
- Genesis 1:3-5
- Genesis 1:6-8
- Genesis 1:9-10
- Genesis 1:11-13
- Genesis 1:14-19
- Genesis 1:20-23
- Genesis 1:24-25
- Genesis 1:26-31
- Genesis 2:1-3

Say: **Open your Bible to your assigned passage and take 30 seconds to discuss with your partner how you might illustrate your passage on this newsprint.** (Pause.)

If I call on your pair, you and your partner will have 30 seconds to illustrate your Scripture verses on the newsprint. (It's OK to use stick figures or other simple drawings.) When your pair isn't drawing, search Genesis 1:1–2:3 with your partner to see if you can figure out which verses are being illustrated. When you've figured it out, stand up. When everyone is standing, we'll read the verses aloud to see if everyone identified the correct passage.

Randomly select a pair to start. Continue giving different pairs the opportunity to draw until all students have had a turn (or until time runs out, whichever comes first).

Afterward, say: **Discuss these questions with your partner:**

- **What went through your mind as you created an illustration of your passage?**
- **How was creating your picture similar to what God did in the creation of the world? How was it different?**
- **Why is it important that God called his creation "good"?**

- **How do you think God felt about creating people? How can you tell?**
- **How do you suppose Adam and Eve felt when God decided he had done a good job creating them?**
- **How does it feel to be something God is proud of making?**

Say: **God looked at everything he made and said, "This is good." When he made you, he said, "This is good!" We are a special part of God's wonderful world.**

Let's find out why God made us so special.

3. Made Just for You

(You'll need paper, pencils, and Bibles.)

Have kids open their Bibles to Genesis 1:1–2:3. Have several volunteers read aloud a few verses until the entire passage has been read.

Next, form groups of no more than four. Say: **In your groups, take turns naming one thing from each day of creation that God knew people would need. Then tell two things from nature that you are especially glad God made.**

After a few minutes of discussion, tell groups to assign the following roles within their foursomes: a recorder who writes down the group's thoughts, a representative who shares the group's thoughts with the class, a reader who reads the Scriptures, and an encourager who urges everyone to participate in the discussion.

(If you have a group of three, have one group member fill two roles. If you have a group of five, have two group members act as encouragers.) Give paper and pencils to the recorders in each group.

Have the readers in each group read

Psalm 139:13-16 aloud. Then ask groups to discuss the following questions:

● **How can you tell that people are a special part of God's creation?**

● **What do you think it means to be made in God's image?**

● **Do you feel like the image of God? Why or why not?**

● **What do Genesis 1:1–2:3 and Psalm 139:13-16 tell us about how we are made?**

● **Why do you think God wanted to communicate to us the story of how we were created?**

When kids are ready, have each group summarize one important thing from its discussion and report it to the class.

Say: **We are a special part of God's wonderful world—even when we don't feel like it. God created us in his image, to be like him in special ways. In our next activity, we'll explore one characteristic God shares with us.**

4. Bubble Gum Creations

(You'll need enough bubble gum for each person to have two pieces, wax paper, and Bibles.)

Say: **God was pretty creative when he made the world. Because we're made in God's image, we have the gift of creativity, too.**

Give each person two pieces of bubble gum and a small square of wax paper. Say: **Chew your gum until it's soft. Then take it out of your mouth and put it on the wax paper. You'll have two minutes to make a creative sculpture to present to the group.** (Let kids with braces who can't chew gum use Silly Putty or modeling clay for their sculptures.)

After two minutes, have each person show his or her sculpture and

explain what it is. Have everyone give a round of applause after each presentation. Ask:

● **What are some of the most unique things you can think of that God created?**

● **As humans, how are we unique?**

● **As an individual, how are you unique?**

Have everyone read Genesis 1:27 together. Ask:

● **How is your creativity like God's creativity?**

Say: **We're a special part of God's wonderful world. In fact, God thinks we're so special that he put some of himself into each of us. When he created us, God added his creative spark in our minds so we, too, can be creative.**

5. Pass It On

(You'll need a bottle of bubbles, a bubble wand, and Bibles.)

Say: **God took great care in making us, and he wants us to care for the amazing world around us. In this relay, we'll practice taking care of something very fragile.**

Form two teams—team A and team B. Have the teams line up, facing each other, about 10 feet apart. Give the first person in team A a bottle of bubbles with a bubble wand. Have that person use the wand to create a bubble, then gently "pass" that bubble through the air (by blowing it) to the first person on team B.

When the bubble reaches team B, have the bubble-blower pop the bubble. Then have team B's first player repeat the process. If a bubble breaks any time during the relay, the appropriate bubble-blower must start again. Allow each bubble-blower no more than two attempts to pass a bubble and award the bubble-blower's team 1 point for each bubble successfully passed.

Have students continue until all team members have had a chance to blow and pass a bubble. If you have more than eight people per team, have students work in pairs as they pass (blow) their bubbles through the air.

Afterward, have the two teams move to the center of the room and face each other. Say: **The person facing you in the other line is now your partner. Discuss my first question with him or her. Then rotate one position to the left for a new partner and answer my next question. If you're at the left end of the line when it's time to rotate, simply move around to the other end. Keep rotating and answering each new question with a new partner.**

Ask:

● **What made this relay difficult?**

● **What went through your mind when your bubble popped before you reached the other team?**

● **What did you do to keep the bubble from popping?**

Have the members of team A read Genesis 1:26, 29, and 30 aloud together. Then ask:

● **What do these verses tell us about our responsibility to the earth?**

● **In what way is our world like the bubble in our relay?**

● **Why is the world sometimes difficult to take care of?**

● **Why should we take care of God's world?**

Say: **We are a special part of God's wonderful world. One of the special jobs God gave us is taking care of this world. Share with your partner one way you can take care of God's world this week. For example, you might set up a bin at home for** recycling glass and cans, or you might "adopt" a block and pick up litter in that block. Make this a goal, not just for this week but for every week.

6. Way to Go, God!

(You'll need newsprint, markers, scissors, and old magazines.)

Say: **Let's have a "Way to Go, God!" party! We'll congratulate God for a job well done and thank God for creating us and the world around us.**

Form two groups. Send one group outside to collect some "creations decorations" such as leaves, flowers, and rocks. (In case of bad weather, have this group make paper cutouts of creation items.) Have the other group stay inside and make a "Thank You!" poster with pictures cut from old magazines of creation items, such as animals, rain, clouds, and mountains.

After five minutes, gather both groups together. Have each person share what he or she is most thankful for in the world. Then say: **God sure made an awesome world, and we are a special part of it! That's worth singing about.**

Lead kids in a time of singing songs about God's creative power, such as "Ah, Lord God," "From the Rising of the Sun," or "Canticle of the Sun." (These songs and many others can be found in *The Group Praise & Worship Songbook* available from Group Publishing.)

7. Thanks, God

Say: **Let's give a prayer of thanks to God for making us a special part of his wonderful world.**

Go outside, form a circle, and join hands. (In case of bad weather, stand under a porch or inside in front of windows.) Say: **Take a good look at the person on your left. Think of one special thing God created about that person. Then be ready to thank God for that special thing in a prayer. For instance, you might say, "Thank you, God, for making Jason with such a great smile" or "Thank you, God, for making Kendra so friendly."**

Go around the circle and have each person pray. After the last person has prayed, have kids shout as loudly as they can, "Thanks, God!"

2. Sin and His Buddy, Consequence
(The First Sin)

The world was still fresh and new when sin entered—bringing with it many unpleasant consequences. Separation from God, pain, struggle, and strife became an ugly part of God's beautiful world. And that was just the beginning.

Today we still live in a sinful world. People sin, often without realizing the serious, life-changing consequences that always accompany their actions. If young people can understand that sin always produces a painful effect, they will make wiser decisions in life. This lesson will help your students realize that sin is always accompanied by consequences.

A POWERFUL POINT

Sin has serious consequences.

A LOOK AT THE LESSON

1. Wash Your Hands, Wash Your Heart (7 minutes)
2. Dear Gabby (8 minutes)
3. Aftershocks (7 minutes)
4. Now You See It . . . (7 minutes)
5. Jingle Bell Relay (8 minutes)
6. The Apple of His Eye (6 minutes)
7. Good for You (6 minutes)

THE FUN-TO-LEARN LESSON

1. Wash Your Hands, Wash Your Heart

(You'll need newspaper, tempera paint, paper plates, doughnuts, soapy water, and paper towels.)

Cover an area of the floor (large enough for your class to stand on) with newspaper. Then pour some water-soluble paint onto a paper plate in the center of your newspaper-covered area. Have kids stand in a circle around the plate.

Say: **We're going to get a little dirty here. I'm going to walk around with this plate of paint, and I want each of you to rub your hands in it. Get them nice and "painty."**

Teacher Tip

This activity can get messy, so caution kids to keep their paint-covered hands over the newspaper.

After everyone has rubbed both hands in the paint, put the paint plate away and bring out the plate of doughnuts. Place the plate in the center of the circle. Say: **Now it's time for some treats! Anyone with clean hands can dig right in!**

Ask:

● **How does it feel to not be able to eat the doughnuts?**

11

● **What's keeping you from them?**

● **What can you do so you'll be able to eat one?**

Bring out a bucket of soapy water and paper towels. Let the kids wash and dry their hands then get a doughnut before going back to their places in the circle. Ask:

● **How is sin in our lives or in our world like the paint on our hands?**

● **What things does sin keep us from doing or having?**

● **How can we wash sin out of our lives?**

Say: **Sin has serious consequences. Today we're going to discover that sin and negative consequences *always* go together. Now let's look at the first sin and the consequences that came with it.**

2. Dear Gabby

(You'll need paper, pencils, and Bibles.)

Form groups of no more than three people. Have each group select a Scripture reader, a secretary, and a reporter. Give each secretary a sheet of paper and a pencil. Have the readers read Genesis 3:1-24 to their groups. Ask:

● **Why do you suppose eating the fruit seemed so appealing to Adam and Eve?**

● **What were some consequences of disobeying God?**

● **How do you suppose Adam and Eve felt when they realized that their sin had serious consequences?**

Say: **I want each group to write a letter from Adam or Eve to "Dear Gabby" for advice about how to deal with the problem of the sin as described in Genesis 3:1-24. Keep the letters short and to the point.**

Be sure everyone in your group contributes some ideas, then have the secretary write the letter. When you're done, exchange letters with another group. Then it's your turn to be Dear Gabby! As a group, answer the letter you've received, giving good advice about how to avoid some bad consequences.

Allow about five minutes for groups to write, exchange, and answer letters. Then have the reporters take turns reading their advice letters. After each letter, ask:

● **How could things have been different for Adam and Eve if they had followed this advice?**

● **What additional advice would you have given?**

● **What advice from this letter can you use in your own life this week?**

Say: **Sin had serious consequences for Adam and Eve, and sin has serious consequences for us today. In our next activity, keep the advice from these letters in mind. Be thinking about how Adam and Eve might have made wiser choices that would have resulted in better consequences.**

3. Aftershocks

(You'll need paper, pencils, newsprint, a marker, and Bibles.)

Have kids scatter around the room and sit down. Hand out paper and pencils. Say: **Write down one sinful action that occurs in the world today. Then, on the back of your paper, write down as many specific consequences of that sin as you can think of. Consider consequences both around the world and close to home.**

For example, you might choose "lying" as the sin to write down.

Some consequences you could list might include **loss of trust in a friendship, disappointment in family members, and hurt feelings.**

After three minutes, bring kids together. On a sheet of newsprint, create two columns labeled "sins" and "consequences." Have kids read aloud what they've written while a volunteer records their responses on the newsprint in the appropriate column.

Read aloud Genesis 3:1-24. Have kids stand as you ask the following questions. Give kids a few seconds to think after each question and tell them you'd like to hear lots of interesting responses. When one student shares an answer, kids who thought of the same answer and have nothing more to add can sit down. When everyone is seated, ask the next question and repeat the process. (If all the kids sit down after the first student shares an answer, have kids stand up and ask the question again to encourage another response.)

Ask:

● **In what way are the consequences of Adam and Eve's sin like the consequences of the sins we've just listed?**

● **How do you think God feels about the sins we've listed?**

● **How do you think God feels when we suffer the consequences of our sins? Why?**

● **Which of the sins and consequences we listed affect you, your family, or kids at your school?** Circle the items that kids mention.

● **Share one way you can work against one of the sins we've circled.** For example, kids might write an encouraging Scripture on their notebooks or pray as they begin each day.

● **What consequences might your actions have?**

● **How will your decision not to sin affect your relationship with God?**

Say: **Sin has serious consequences. Adam and Eve were the first to realize this truth. Looking at our list, you can see how bad and how far-reaching those consequences can be! Let's keep that list up for the rest of our lesson as a reminder of all the negative effects of sin.**

4. Now You See It...

(You'll need toothpicks, paper, a lemon or a cup of lemon juice, a lamp without a shade, and Bibles.)

Form groups of four. Give everyone a toothpick and a piece of paper. Give each group a small piece of lemon or a small cup of lemon juice. Have the kids use the toothpicks and lemon juice to write their names on their papers. As the "ink" dries, have the groups read Genesis 3:1-8 among themselves. Direct students to number off within their groups from one to four.

Say: **Discuss the next few questions in your groups. Then I'll call out a number from one to four. The person in your group whose number I call out will be responsible for sharing your answer.**

Ask:

● **Why do you think Adam and Eve tried to hide from God when he asked about their sin?**

● **What would have been a better response?**

● **What do you think you would have done if you had been Adam or Eve?**

● **What are some ways we try to "hide" from God when we sin?**

● **How does hiding our sins affect the consequences of those sins?**

● **What would be a better response than trying to hide our sins?**

Turn on a lamp without a shade. Have volunteers bring their papers up and hold them close to the light bulb of the lamp. After a few seconds, the lemon juice will turn brown and become very visible.

Ask:

● **How is the lemon juice like sin?**

● **Why can't we hide our sins?**

● **How should we deal with our sins?**

Say: **Sin has serious consequences. Even when no one sees the sin, we can't hide our sin because the consequences are always visible! That's why it's important to confess our sins, rather than try to hide or cover them up. Let's explore how sin and consequences are tied together.**

5. Jingle Bell Relay

(You'll need two chairs, two jingle bells, and two ribbons.)

Form two teams and have the teams form two single-file lines at one end of the room. At the other end of the room, place a chair opposite each team. Give the first person on each team a jingle bell attached to a ribbon.

Say: **When I give the signal, tie the ribbon to your ankle, run as fast as you can to the chair, touch it, then run back and give the jingle bell to the next person in line. And you have to do all of that without allowing the jingle bell to make *any* noise! If it does, you have to start over again. Ready, set, go!**

Throughout the relay, have kids keep their cheering soft so everyone can hear any jingling. When the last person has finished, have the two teams face each other.

Say: **The person facing you in the**

other line is now your partner. Discuss my first question with him or her. Then rotate one position to the left for a new partner and answer my next question. If you're at the left end of the line when it's time to rotate, simply move around to the other end. Keep rotating and answering each new question with a new partner.

Ask:

● **How did you feel trying to keep the jingle bell quiet during this relay?**

● **How did the jingle bell affect the way you ran the relay?**

● **How did the consequences of the bell ringing affect your team?**

● **How was the jingle bell and its ringing like sin and its consequences?**

● **How do the consequences of sin affect you?**

● **How do the consequences of sin affect those around you?**

● **What is one negative consequence you could avoid this week by resisting sin?**

Say: **Sin has serious consequences that usually affect more than one person. Just like you couldn't run without the bell ringing, you can't sin without some consequence. Even though our sins have lasting effects, it's encouraging to know that God forgives our sins. We'll explore that idea in our next activity.**

6. The Apple of His Eye

(You'll need an apple and Bibles.)

Form a large circle. Select four volunteers to read Genesis 3 in the following sections: 3:1-7; 3:8-13; 3:14-20; and 3:21-24. Then say: **Although we can't erase the consequences of our sins, we know that God forgives** every sin. **All we have to do is ask! Sometimes when we're suffering the effects of our sins, it's hard to remember that God has wiped them away.**

Give someone an apple and have that person read John 3:16-17. Then have the person gently toss the apple to someone else and say, "God forgave (name)," filling in the second person's name. Have kids continue to gently toss the apple around until everyone's name has been said. Have the last person read John 3:16-17 aloud, then silently erase the sins written on the chalkboard in the "Aftershocks" activity.

7. Good For You

(You'll need an apple, newsprint, and a marker.)

Form pairs. Cut an apple into enough pieces so that everyone has at least a bite.

Say: **I'm going to give each of you a piece of apple, but don't eat it yet. After you and your partner both have your apple pieces, think** of three good things that come from eating an apple. For example, dentists say that eating an apple can help clean harmful plaque off your teeth.

Allow a few minutes for partners to discuss ideas, then have the older partner of each pair share that pair's ideas with the class.

Say: **Just as bad actions have bad consequences, good actions have good consequences. With your partner, think of three good actions you could take this week that would lead to good consequences.**

Allow a few minutes for partners to discuss ideas, then have the younger partner in each pair report that pair's ideas to the class. Write kids' ideas on newsprint for everyone to see.

Say: **Take a few minutes and pray with your partner that God will help you make good decisions that lead to good actions and good consequences. Then eat your apples as a symbol of the good that God can do in your lives.**

3. Have Faith and Follow
(God Tests Abraham)

"Take your only son, Isaac, the son you love, and go to the land of Moriah. Kill him there and offer him as a whole burnt offering..." (Genesis 22:2). Imagine how you might have felt. "Are you crazy, God? This is my son! Sarah and I waited years for this baby! Sacrifice Isaac? You must be kidding!" But not Abraham. He didn't cry, whine, beg, plead, question, or even flinch. He got up early the next morning and did exactly as God asked.

It's not often that God asks us to do something so drastic. But if he were to ask, would we obey? A rock-solid trust in God takes time to develop. That's why fourth grade and up can be a crucial time for young Christians. This is when they often begin to experience what it means to trust and follow God. This lesson will give students insight into the importance of trusting and following God.

A POWERFUL POINT

God wants us to trust and follow him.

A LOOK AT THE LESSON

1. Following My Leader (5 minutes)
2. On Your Toes (7 minutes)
3. Bible Blender (10 minutes)
4. Pay to Play (9 minutes)
5. Footprints (8 minutes)
6. My Sacrifice (6 minutes)

THE FUN-TO-LEARN LESSON

1. Following My Leader

Form a line and lead the group around the room. You may want to add a few simple motions—similar to the game Follow the Leader. Then turn out the lights and lead the group around the room. (If your classroom doesn't get very dark, have kids close their eyes.) Call out a few instructions such as "Hop backward four times," "Put your hands in the air," or "Walk very slowly." Turn on the lights, form a circle, and ask:

● **How did you feel just now when you were following me?**

● **What were some difficulties you had when the lights were out? How did you handle the difficulties?**

● **Which experience was more like following God? Explain.**

Say: **God wants us to trust and follow him. Trusting and following God would be easy if we always knew where he was leading us, but often we don't know. Today we're going to look at someone in the Bible who had to trust and follow God—even when it seemed God was leading him the wrong way.**

2. On Your Toes

(You'll need photocopies of the "Daffy Directions" handout on page 20 and Bibles.)

Give kids copies of the "Daffy Directions" handout. Say: **When I give the signal to begin, follow the directions on the sheet. Be sure to do each one and try to do it well.**

Tell kids to start, then watch the bedlam. When everyone has completed the list, form a circle and ask:

● **How did you feel while you were acting out the directions on your list? Why did you feel that way?**

● **Would you have felt different if the directions had been less silly? Explain.**

● **Why did you act out your list?**

Form two circles, one within the other. Have the members of the inner circle face outward and the members of the outer circle face inward so kids are facing each other. Have the kids in the inner circle read Genesis 22:1-10 aloud together. Say: **The person facing you is now your partner. Discuss my first question with him or her, then move to the right to get a new partner for the next question**. Ask:

● **How do you suppose Abraham felt when God gave him these directions?**

● **What evidence do you have that Abraham trusted God?**

● **What evidence is there in your life that you trust God?**

● **Give some modern examples of times when God's directions seem strange or difficult. Try to think of something specific, like bringing a friend to church, obeying your parents, or doing your best in school.**

● **Why is it difficult for you to do that one thing?**

Have the kids in the outer circle read Genesis 22:11-19 aloud together. Ask:

● **What great things came from Abraham trusting and obeying God?**

● **What great things can happen when you trust in and obey God?**

● **Why should we obey God when his directions seem strange or hard to us? What happens if we don't obey God?**

● **How might the story have been different if Abraham hadn't trusted God?**

● **What area in your life might be different if you completely trust God with it?**

Say: **God blessed Abraham because Abraham trusted in God and obeyed God's commands even when they didn't seem to make sense. God wants us to trust and follow him, too. Let's look at some other people in the Bible who faced the decision to obey or not to obey.**

3. Bible Blender

(You'll need paper, pencils, and Bibles.)

Form four groups and assign each group one of the following passages:

● Joshua 7:10-26
● Jonah 1
● Genesis 6:11-22; 8:15-20
● Joshua 6:1-20

Hand out paper and pencils to each person. Say: **Work together on the following assignment. Be sure everyone jots down your group's answers because in a few minutes each of you will share your ideas with a new group.**

Have groups read their passages and complete the following assignments:

● **Summarize the story in your passage.**

● **List the rewards that came from obeying God.**

● **List the consequences that resulted from disobeying God.**

When everyone is finished, have

kids number off within their groups from one to however many kids are in the group. Have all the ones form a new group, all the twos, and so on. Each new group should have one member from each of the four original groups. Have kids each summarize and share the consequences and rewards from the passages that their original group read.

When everyone is done, say: **In your group, brainstorm some of the serious consequences that stem from disobeying God today. For example, people who have sex outside of marriage risk the consequences of AIDS or unwanted pregnancies. Choose one person in your group to record your ideas on paper and another to report them to the class.**

Allow two or three minutes of brainstorming, then have a reporter from each group share the list aloud.

Say: **God wants us to trust and follow him. God rewards people who follow him, but sometimes following God requires sacrifice. Let's explore the cost of following God.**

4. Pay to Play

(You'll need candy, tennis balls, a chalkboard and chalk, and Bibles.)

Give each student a piece of candy but instruct kids not to eat the candy yet. Form pairs and give each pair a tennis ball. Have partners stand side to side, holding the tennis ball between their shoulders. Say: **This is a basic game of Tag. I'm going to choose two pairs to be "It." If they tag you, you and your partner must freeze until another pair can tag and free you. If you drop your tennis ball, you and your partner must freeze until another pair "unfreezes" you. Every once in a while, I'll blow the whistle. If you and your partner are frozen when I blow the whistle, you're It! If you and your partner are It when I blow the whistle, you aren't It anymore. Oh, and everyone has to pay one piece of candy to play this game.**

Collect the candy, then play the game for about five minutes. Then have kids sit down and discuss the following questions with their partners:

● **How did you feel about giving up your candy to play the game?**

● **Was that a high price to pay for a game of Tag? Explain.**

● **What were the rewards of playing the game?**

Have pairs read Genesis 22:1-19 together. Ask:

● **What is the cost of following God?**

● **What are the rewards of following God?**

Have pairs share their responses to the last question with the class. Write their responses on the chalkboard. If necessary, help kids refine or elaborate on the ideas to make them specific and applicable to their age level. For example, "happiness" could be expanded to "happiness in knowing that you are pleasing God."

Say: **Choose one item from this list of rewards that you would like your partner to receive. Then give your partner a piece of candy and say, "As you trust and follow God, may you receive** (name the reward).**"**

Hand out candy, then have partners exchange candy and reward wishes.

Say: **God wants us to trust and follow him. When you trust and follow God, you're doing what God knows is best for you. Let's look at some steps we can take to follow God.**

5. Footprints

(You'll need construction paper, markers, scissors, and tape.)

Form groups of three and have all the groups stand at one end of the room. Say: **Your goal is to get your trio across the room in a creative and fun way. You have two minutes to plan how you'll do it. Maybe you'll want to make a wheelbarrow out of the people in your group or have everyone do backward somersaults across the floor. This isn't a race, so be creative and have fun!**

After about two minutes, call on one trio at a time to cross the room. After everyone has crossed the room, have kids discuss the following questions in their trios:

● **What made your method of crossing the room fun?**

● **What is your reaction to making a simple goal—like crossing the room—fun?**

● **How would taking a creative approach to reaching goals affect your attitude toward those goals?**

● **How would taking a creative approach to following God affect your relationship with God?**

Hand out construction paper, markers, and scissors. Have students each trace their feet on the construction paper and cut out the footprints.

Say: **Work together as a trio to think of creative steps you can take to reach the goal of trusting and following God. Sometimes giving a wacky twist to something you know you should do makes that action more fun and easier to remember to do. For instance, one step toward following God is reading your Bible regularly. A creative twist on that would be to read a chapter in the bathtub every time you take a bath.**

Have kids write a creative idea on each footprint. Then let them share their ideas with the class and tape their footprints on the wall. Have kids sign their initials on at least one footprint to indicate they'll put that idea into practice this week.

Say: **God wants us to trust and follow him. Planning what steps we'll take is a good way to get started. When we're creative about taking those steps, we can have a lot of fun. But trusting and obeying God may also take sacrifice. Let's see what God may be asking you to sacrifice or give to him.**

6. My Sacrifice

(You'll need paper, pencils, and Bibles.)

Hand out paper and pencils. In trios, have kids read Genesis 22:1-19, then share something that would be hard for them to give to God. That something might be a possession, an emotion, a relationship, or a person. Have each member write what they shared on a piece of paper. Place a chair or table at one end of the room.

Say: **God may never ask you to give up the thing that's most important to you. But if you really trust God and want to follow him, you need to be willing to give your precious person or thing to him—just as Abraham was willing to give up Isaac. This chair is like an altar to God. Let's put our papers on the chair as a symbol of turning over our treasures to God. Use this as a time of silent prayer to God.**

Have kids silently lay their papers on the chair.

1 Sing "Mary Had a Little Lamb."

2 Count to 100 by tens.

3 Touch your tongue to your nose.

4 Cross your eyes.

5 Form a circle with at least two other people and shout "Hey!" all together.

6 Do the wave with at least three other people.

7 Cheer, "Hip, Hip, Hooray!" three times.

8 Do five jumping jacks.

9 Untie and retie your shoelaces.

Permission to photocopy this handout from *Fun-to-Learn Bible Lessons: Grades 4 & Up* granted for local church use. Copyright © Group Publishing, Inc., Box 481, Loveland, CO 80539.

4. The Green-Eyed Monster (Joseph and His Brothers)

Jealousy is a dangerous emotion. It can lead people to do the unthinkable. Just ask Joseph, whose brothers were so envious of him that they sold him to a band of gypsies! Although most of us have never gone to such measures, all of us have felt the painful twinges of jealousy at one time or another.

Children experience the pain of jealousy, too. Whether it's envy of material possessions or emotional attentions, jealousy is a very real emotion to upper-elementary kids. They need to learn how to handle this powerful emotion. Use this lesson to help students explore jealousy and its effects and to challenge them with positive ways to handle envy.

A POWERFUL POINT

With God's help, we can overcome jealousy.

A LOOK AT THE LESSON

1. When Life Gives You Lemons (6 minutes)

2. Oh, Brother! (8 minutes)

3. Joseph and the Corvette (9 minutes)

4. Locked In (6 minutes)

5. Your Coat of Many Colors (8 minutes)

6. Help Hot Line (8 minutes)

THE FUN-TO-LEARN LESSON

1. When Life Gives You Lemons

(You'll need lemon wedges and damp cloths or hand wipes.)

Form a circle and give each person a lemon wedge. Have everyone lick the lemon slice or, better yet, take a bite of it.

Say: **Describe how the lemon tastes.**

Next, have kids rub the lemons over their hands. Ask:

● **How does the lemon juice feel?**

● **How can you get rid of that feeling?**

Say: **Today we're going to talk about jealousy. Take a minute and think of a time when you felt jealous.** (Pause.)

Ask: **How is the lemon juice like the feeling of jealousy?**

After many students have answered, say: **Jealousy is an unpleasant feeling that can lead to unhappiness. But with God's help, we can overcome jealousy. Today we're going to look at someone whose life changed because his brothers were envious of him.**

Teacher Tip

Some students may like the way the lemon juice tastes or feels—and that's OK. Use that as a teachable moment to help kids explore why people sometimes like feelings of jealousy or why they sometimes like to make others jealous.

Hand out damp cloths or hand wipes and have kids wash their hands before moving to the next activity.

2. Oh, Brother!

(You'll need paper, pencils, and Bibles.)

Form three groups and give each group a piece of paper and a pencil. Have each group elect a secretary then read Genesis 37:1-8, 18-36. Allow 30 seconds for groups to search for and write down as many things as they can find that Joseph's brothers envied. Then have each group act out what they wrote while the other groups guess what they are acting out.

Form three new groups and have each group select a secretary. Then have groups read Genesis 37:18-31. Allow 30 seconds for groups to search for and write down as many things as they can find that Joseph's brothers did because of jealousy. Then have each group act out what they wrote while the other groups guess.

When all the groups have acted out their lists, form a circle and choose someone to read Genesis 37:31-36. Have kids stand as you ask the following questions. Give kids a moment to think after each question and tell them you'd like to hear lots of interesting responses.

When one student shares an answer, kids who thought of the same answer and have nothing more to add can sit down. When everyone is seated, ask the next question and repeat the process. (If all the kids sit down after the first student shares an answer, have kids stand up and ask the question again to encourage another response.)

Ask:
● **If you had been one of Joseph's brothers, how do you think you would have felt?**
● **How do you think you would have handled your emotions?**
● **How could Joseph's brothers have handled their emotions better?**
● **What makes you jealous?**
● **How can you handle your jealousy?**

Say: **Joseph's brothers let their jealousy lead them to do evil things that caused everyone a lot of pain. God loves us so much that he wants to help us avoid that kind of pain. With God's help, we can overcome jealousy.**

3. Joseph and the Corvette

(You'll need paper, pencils, and Bibles.)

Say: **You may think you don't have trouble with jealousy because you've never tried to sell your siblings into slavery. But let's think about what the story of Joseph would be like in a more modern setting.**

Form groups of four. Have each group select two Scripture readers, a secretary, and a reporter. Give each secretary a sheet of paper and a pencil. Have the first readers read Genesis 37:1-8 and the second readers read Genesis 37:18-36 to their groups.

Ask:
● **What are people jealous of today?**

● **In your group, share a time when you were jealous. What made you feel that way?**

● **How do people deal with their envy today?**

Say: **Take a few minutes and rewrite the story you read in Genesis, except set it in today's society. What would Joseph's brothers be jealous of, what would they do, and what might the result be? Be creative but also try to think realistically.**

Allow two to three minutes for groups to come up with a story and have the secretary write the story down. Then have the reporters from each group read their stories. Ask:

● **Are the results of jealousy any different now than they were in Bible times? Explain.**

● **How does Jesus' life and death change how we deal with jealousy?**

Say: **Jealousy causes so much pain. But with God's help, we can overcome jealousy and be free of that pain. God loves each of us so much that he sent Jesus to die, freeing us from all sin—including envy! Let's explore how jealousy is like a trap that we need to be released from.**

4. Locked In

Form two groups—group A and group B. Have group A form a circle around group B and link arms tightly. Then have the members of group B try to escape from the circle. (Remind kids to be gentle—no hitting, pinching, kicking, or shoving allowed!) After one minute have groups switch roles and give the members of group A one minute to escape.

Have the members of group A form a circle inside group B and face outward. Have the members of group B face inward so kids are facing each other.

Say: **The person facing you is now your partner. Discuss my first question with him or her and then move to the right to get a new partner for the next question.**

Ask:

● **What was it like to be inside the circle?**

● **How is that feeling like the feeling of jealousy?**

● **How did jealousy trap Joseph's brothers?**

● **How might jealousy trap you?**

● **What is one area in which you need Jesus to free you from the trap of jealousy this week?**

Say: **With God's help we can overcome jealousy and break free from its trap. Stay with the partner you just shared with and pray together quietly, asking God to help your partner break free from the trap of jealousy this week. When you're done praying, wait quietly until everyone else is done. When you hear me say "amen," everyone shout together "AMEN!" and break the circle apart.**

5. Your Coat of Many Colors

(You'll need paper grocery bags, colored markers, and scissors.)

Say: **It's easy to find things to envy about other people. But now you're going to find out some of the great things other people see in you.**

Give each person a large paper bag and a colored marker. Instruct kids to make a vest out of the bag by cutting a hole on each thin side (for arms), a hole at the bottom of the bag (for the head), and a straight line starting at the head opening and continuing down the front of the bag. Have kids put on their vests. (If you have time, have kids decorate their vests by drawing pockets, buttons, or other designs on them.)

Say: **We're going to create coats of many colors! For the next few minutes, go around and write some great affirming messages on each other's paper-bag "coats." Think of something you can write that will really make someone feel special. For example, you might write, "I love your smile" for someone who is friendly and welcoming or "You have a great sense of humor" for someone who makes you laugh.**

After each person has had a chance to write on everyone else's coat, form a circle and ask:

● **What emotions did this experience bring out in you? Explain.**

● **How could affirming someone help that person deal with jealousy?**

● **What are some ways God encourages you and makes you feel special?**

● **How can that help you deal with jealous feelings?**

● **What could you do to make someone feel special this week?**

Say: **Take your coats home and keep them as reminders of how**

special you are to others. Whenever jealous feelings come your way, put your coat on to protect yourself from those dangerous emotions! With God's help, we can overcome jealousy.

6. Help Hot Line

(You'll need yellow construction paper, ordinary yellow or white paper, markers, stapler, and Bibles.)

Form pairs. Hand out one sheet of yellow construction paper, one sheet of ordinary yellow or white paper, and a marker to each person.

Say: **Many phone books list emergency hot lines in the yellow pages. You and your partner are going to make your own yellow pages for a jealousy help hot line.**

Show kids how to fold their papers in half and place the ordinary paper inside the yellow construction paper to form a booklet with four pages inside. Pass around a stapler so kids can staple their booklets on the fold.

Say: **Read the following passages and then work as a pair to create a "yellow pages" listing for each passage—one listing per page. For example, for Genesis 1:27 you might write, "Jealousy—Personal" in the upper corner of the page. Then write a sentence like "If you're feeling jealous because**

someone seems better than you, remember that you are made in God's image." Next, write out the verse and its reference.

You can use any format you want, but be sure to write out each passage and its reference.

Assign the following passages: Genesis 1:27; James 3:14-16; Psalm 139:14-16; and Psalm 49:16-17.

When the pairs have completed their booklets, ask:

● **How might these passages help you when you're feeling jealous?**

Have each person choose one of the verses to learn for next week.

Say: **With God's help, we can overcome jealousy. Put your yellow pages to work this week. Everyone, call your partner sometime this week to encourage that person and see how he or she is coming on remembering the verse. Next week, share your verse with us and update the class on how it influenced you during the week.**

5. Mission Is-Possible . . . With God, That Is!
(The Burning Bush)

The world is full of problems. Famine, homelessness, gang wars, drugs, injustice, and corruption can make life seem pretty dismal at times. Moses' world wasn't so pleasant, either. The Egyptians, ruled by a foul Pharaoh, were using the Israelites (yes, God's chosen people) as slaves. But when God called upon Moses to free his people, Moses wasn't so sure he was the man for the job. How could a mere shepherd save his nation? A quick read through the book of Exodus shows us that a shepherd could and did do just that—with help from a powerful and wise God.

How often do we feel like Moses, very small against the enormity of the task God has placed before us? Yet how often have we seen God use the most ordinary person to do the most extraordinary feat? Upper-elementary kids can feel that way, too. The problems of the world around them seem so enormous, so out of control, that for one person to make a difference seems impossible. But with God's help, their mission IS possible! This lesson will help students see that with God's help, they can do anything!

A POWERFUL POINT

God can use each of us in unique and powerful ways.

A LOOK AT THE LESSON

1. Tug o' What? (7 minutes)
2. Empower Me (8 minutes)
3. Miracles for Moses (7 minutes)
4. Crazy Cotton Competition (10 minutes)
5. Ordinary Joes (8 minutes)
6. Seeds (9 minutes)

THE FUN-TO-LEARN LESSON

1. Tug o' What?

(You'll need about 10 feet of sturdy rope.)

Form two teams, A and B. Have each team take hold of an end of the rope and compete in a game of Tug of War. Then have team A play against half of team B. Next, switch roles and have all of team B play against half of team A. Then have everyone play a normal game of Tug of War. Afterward, have kids sit down in a circle. Then ask:

● **What did you think when I took away half of your team?**

● **How did it feel to have the other half of your team back?**

● **How is getting your whole team back like the extra power that God gives us?**

● **Why does having God in your life give you added strength?**

● **What kind of strength does God give you?**

Say: **God gives us extra power—the power to do things we never** thought we could do. Today we're going to discover how God can use us in unique and powerful ways. First let's read about a man who God asked to do an enormous task: save his entire nation!

2. Empower Me

(You'll need photocopies of the "But, God!" handout on page 31).

Form trios and hand out copies of the "But, God!" handout based on Exodus 3:1–4:17. Have kids read the script within their trios, each person taking one part. Then have the kids discuss the following questions within their trios:

● **How would you feel if God gave you a massive assignment like Moses' assignment?**

● **How do you think God felt when Moses tried to get out of his assignment?**

● **Share one thing you would like to accomplish with God's help.**

● **How do you feel about facing your task?**

● **How is that like the way Moses felt?**

● **What could God tell you that would help you accomplish what you want to do?**

Say: **Despite Moses' doubts about his own ability, God used Moses to do great things. God can use each of us in unique and powerful ways. Let's look more closely at how God works through people.**

3. Miracles for Moses

(You'll need Bibles.)

Form groups of four and direct students to number off within their groups from one to four.

Say: **During this discussion time, I'll be asking questions for your groups to talk about. Then I'll call**

out a number from one to four. The person in your group whose number I call out will be responsible for sharing your group's answer.

For example, after the first question, I might call out the number "three." Each person assigned the number three will be responsible for reporting his or her group's answer to the class.

Have all the ones read Exodus 3:7-9 to their groups. Then begin discussion by asking:

● **What does this passage tell us about God?**

● **Do you see God that way today? Explain.**

Have all the twos read Exodus 3:2-4 and 4:2-7 to their groups. Ask:

● **Why did God show Moses these miracles?**

● **What do they tell us about God?**

● **Do you see God that way today? In what way?**

Have all the threes read Exodus 3:10-16 and 4:10-13 to their groups. Ask:

● **What do you think Moses was afraid of?**

● **Share a time when you've been afraid.**

● **How can the things we've read in the previous verses help you overcome those feelings?**

Have all the fours read Exodus 4:14-16 to their groups. Ask:

● **Why do you think God was angry with Moses' reaction?**

● **Should Moses have trusted God more? Explain.**

● **In what areas do you need to trust God more?**

● **Share one way that you can show your trust in God this week.**

Say: **God can use us in unique and powerful ways, but only if we allow him to! Moses had many reasons for God to choose someone** else, but God knew Moses was the perfect man for the job. Let's explore some reasons why people don't allow God to use them.

4. Crazy Cotton Competition

(You'll need blindfolds, cotton balls, newsprint, a marker, and tape.)

Form two teams, A and B. Have them form two lines at one end of the room. Give the first person in each line a blindfold and a cotton ball.

Say: **When I give the signal, put on the blindfold, get on your hands and knees, and blow the cotton ball to the other end of the room. The rest of your team will be with you all the way, giving you directions. When you get to the other end of the room, you can take off your blindfold, grab the cotton ball, and race back to this end of the room. Then give the blindfold and the cotton ball to the next person in line.**

Have kids run the relay. Afterward, have the two teams move to the center of the room and face each other. Say: **The person facing you in the other line is now your partner. Discuss my first question with him or her. Then rotate one position to the left for a new partner and answer my next question. If you're at the left end of the line when it's time to rotate, simply move around to the other end. Keep rotating and answering each new question with a new partner.**

Ask:

● **How did you feel about performing this relay?**

● **What are some reasons you didn't want to do the relay or thought you wouldn't be able to do the relay well?**

● **How are these excuses like the excuses we give when God asks us to do something difficult?**

● **If God asked you to do one thing to improve our community this week, what excuses would you be likely to give?**

● **How do you think God might respond to those excuses?**

● **What would the relay have been like without the help of your team members?**

● **What would life be like without God's support?**

● **How can God help you overcome your excuses this week?**

Tape a sheet of newsprint to the wall. Say: **Raise your hand when you've thought of an answer to the next question. I'd like to hear lots of different, interesting answers. When you've given an answer, you may lower your hand. If someone gives an answer you've thought of and you don't have anything more to add, you may lower your hand, too.**

Ask: **What is something you can do, with God's help, to improve our community?** Help kids think of specific actions they can take, such as taking blankets to a homeless shelter, getting a group together to pick up trash around the school, making cards and taking them to a local children's hospital, cleaning up graffiti, or inviting their soccer team to church. As each person responds, write the suggestion on the newsprint.

When everyone has given at least one suggestion, have kids sign their initials next to the one idea they'll try to accomplish this week. (Consider organizing a group project to give your students the experience of accomplishing something for God.) The next time you meet, allow a few minutes for kids to report on their projects.

Say: **We can give God a thousand excuses why he shouldn't use us. But with the support of such a powerful God, those excuses seem pretty weak. God can use anyone of any age, size, intelligence, or ability. God can use each of us in unique and powerful ways. Whether it's blowing a cotton ball or moving a mountain, with God's help... you can do it!**

5. Ordinary Joes

(You'll need paper, pencils, and Bibles.)

Form four groups and assign each group one of the following passages:
● 1 Samuel 17
● Joshua 6:1-21
● Luke 1:26-38
● Joshua 2:1-17; 6:22-25

Give each person a piece of paper and a pencil. Say: **Read your verses and answer my questions. Make sure everyone in your group writes down your answers because in a few minutes you'll share your responses with someone from one of the other groups.**

Ask:

● **How did God use the person in your passage?**

● **What was the person's reaction to God?**

● **How did God help this person?**

Have kids number off within their groups, starting with the number one and ending with the total number of kids in their groups. Then form new discussion groups by having kids with the same number gather together. For example, all the ones form a new group, all the twos form another group, and so on. Have kids tell their new groups about the passages they read and then give their answers. Ask:

● **Why do you think God uses**

ordinary people to do extraordinary things?

● **How do you feel about God using you to do extraordinary things? Explain.**

Say: **God can use each of us in unique and powerful ways. God has always used the average to accomplish the amazing. As we close, let's take a look at how God does the same thing in nature.**

6. Seeds

(You'll need a packet of marigold seeds, paper cups, markers or pens, and potting soil.)

Seat kids in a circle. Pour a few marigold seeds in your hand and walk around the circle, allowing each person to get a good look at the seeds. Ask each person to say one word that describes the seeds. Then tell kids that these are marigold seeds (you may want to show them a picture of marigolds). Have each person say one word that describes what the marigolds will look like in a month. Ask:

● **How are we like seeds right now?**

● **How can God help us "bloom"?**

Give each person a paper cup and a marker. Say: **God can use each of us in unique and powerful ways. God is already working in your life to make you like a beautiful and productive plant. Write your name on your paper cup, then pass it to the person on your left.**

Now write one word that describes something good about the person whose cup you're holding. Think of positive adjectives like dynamic, resourceful, sensitive, and kind. Keep passing the cups around and writing on them until you get your own cup back.

When the cups have gone all the way around the circle, provide potting soil and marigold seeds and have kids plant seeds in their cups.

Say: **Take your cup home and give the seeds plenty of water and light. Soon you should have plants and then flowers. Whenever you look at your flowers, remember that God can do great things from just a tiny seed. Also, remember that God can use each of us in unique and powerful ways.**

But, God!

Narrator: While Moses was tending his father-in-law's sheep, he led them to a place called Sinai, the mountain of God. There Moses saw an angel of the Lord within the flames of a burning bush. God called to Moses from within the bush.

God: Moses, I have seen the misery of my people in Egypt. I have heard them crying out because of their slave drivers, and I am concerned about their suffering. So I have come down to rescue them from the hand of the Egyptians and to bring them into a good, spacious land—a land flowing with milk and honey. I am sending you to Pharaoh to bring my people out of Egypt.

Moses: Who am I that I should go to Pharaoh and bring the Israelites out of Egypt?

God: I will be with you.

Moses: What if I go to the Israelites and tell them, "The God of your fathers has sent me to you," and they ask me, "What is his name?" What shall I tell them?

God: Say, "The Lord, the God of your fathers—Abraham, Isaac, and Jacob—has sent me to you."

Moses: What if they do not believe me or listen to me? What if they say, "The Lord did not appear to you"?

God: Take your staff and throw it on the ground.

Narrator: Moses threw his staff on the ground and it became a snake, and he ran from it.

God: Reach out and take it by the tail.

Narrator: So Moses took hold of the snake's tail, and it turned back into a staff.

God: This is so they may believe that the Lord has appeared to you.

Moses: But, Lord, I've never been eloquent. I am slow of speech and tongue.

God: Who gave man his mouth? Who makes him deaf and dumb? Who gives him sight or makes him blind? Is it not I, the Lord? Now go, I will help you speak and teach you what to say.

Moses: Oh, Lord, please send someone else to do it.

Narrator: Then the Lord's anger burned against Moses.

God: What about your brother Aaron? He can speak well. He is on his way to meet you. You shall speak to him and put words in his mouth; I will help both of you speak and will teach you what to do. He will speak to the people for you, and it will be as if he were your mouth.

Permission to photocopy this handout from *Fun-to-Learn Bible Lessons: Grades 4 & Up* granted for local church use. Copyright © Group Publishing, Inc., Box 481, Loveland, CO 80539.

6. Risky Rewards of Faith (Rahab)

Life can be risky for kids. They are faced with temptations every day. Big decisions that will change their lives forever are around every corner. Faith is the key that can unlock their potential while closing out the things that can hurt them. Faith can be risky, too. But the rewards are awesome. The story of Rahab presents life and death risks with obvious rewards.

Kids want to know what's in it for them. They are aware of some of the risks in life. Use this lesson to let them know that God can bless them as they put their faith to work.

A POWERFUL POINT

When you trust God, the rewards outweigh the risks.

A LOOK AT THE LESSON

1. Do What's Right (8 minutes)
2. Spies in the City (8 minutes)
3. Real-Life Rahabs (9 minutes)
4. What's the Question? (15 minutes)
5. Spies and Soldiers (7 minutes)
6. Red Ribbons (7 minutes)

THE FUN-TO-LEARN LESSON

1. Do What's Right

(You'll need photocopies of the "What Would You Do?" handout on page 36, paper, and pencils.)

Say: **Today we're going to be talking about the risks and rewards of faith. To start, let's explore some risky situations.**

Form groups of no more than three. Have each group select a reader, a secretary, and a reporter. Give each secretary a sheet of paper and a pencil. Give each trio a copy of one of the situations from the "What Would You Do?" handout.

> ### Teacher Tip
>
> If you have fewer groups than situations, simply choose the ones that are most compelling for the kids in your class. It's OK if you don't use all the situations on the handout. If you have more than five groups, allow some threesomes to discuss the same situation.

Have the reader in each group read the situation and the questions following it. Have the trios discuss the questions while the secretary records their responses. When all the groups have finished, have the reporters from each group share their situations and responses with the class.

Say: **It can be risky to live as Jesus wants us to. But when you trust God, the rewards outweigh the risks. Let's find out about a woman who knew about both the risks and the rewards of trusting God.**

2. Spies in the City

(You'll need chalk, a chalkboard, and Bibles.)

Have kids interject responses as you read the Bible story aloud. Before you read the passage, ask:

● **How would you describe "bad guys" in today's terms?**

● **What would you say about "good guy" spies?**

Write the suggestions on the chalkboard, then choose one response as the answer for each question in the following story. For example, you might choose the word "mean" as a response to indicate bad guys and "honest" as a response to indicate good guys. Erase the other words from the chalkboard and rewrite the chosen words in big print.

Hand out Bibles. Say: **As I read aloud the story of Rahab and the spies, follow along and respond using the words on the board. When you hear "the men" mentioned in the verses, ask out loud, "What men?" Then when we know if they're the good guys or the bad guys, use the appropriate word from the board.**

Read aloud Joshua 2:1-15, 18 and 6:16-17, encouraging kids to interject the words describing the men. Afterward, ask:

● **Everyone wearing black, answer this question: If you had been Rahab, what would have gone through your mind when the king's men came looking for the spies?**

● **Everyone wearing green, answer this question: What do you think would have happened to Rahab if she had been caught hiding the spies?**

● **Everyone wearing a belt, answer this question: How did what Rahab knew about God influ-**ence her decision to take the risk? **Refer to Joshua 2:9-13 for help in discussing your answer.**

● **Everyone wearing red, answer this question: What do you know about God that gives you the confidence to take risks?**

Say: **Rahab learned that when you trust God the rewards outweigh the risks. Rahab was allowed to live, and so was her whole family. Let's explore some of the risks and rewards of trusting God in our everyday lives.**

3. Real-Life Rahabs

(You'll need paper and pencils.)

Form groups of three. Say: **Rahab faced a life and death situation. The risks were obvious and so was the reward. In everyday life the risks aren't always as great. And sometimes it can be hard to recognize the rewards.**

We're going to write our own stories of risks and rewards and make the setting realistic for our lives. Each group will write a story about someone your age who faces a real-life risk for living like a Christian.

Try to identify a realistic risk anybody might face, even if it's not dramatic. For instance, your hero might have to decide whether to risk popularity by befriending somebody the other kids pick on. What rewards might your hero get for living out his or her faith in that way?

Have each group appoint an encourager, a scribe, and a reporter. The encourager will urge each person to contribute to the story. The scribe will record ideas and write the final story. The reporter will read the story to the class. Give each scribe a sheet of paper and a pencil.

Allow five minutes for each group

to work. Give a two-minute warning at the appropriate time. When all the groups are ready, let reporters present their stories to the class. After each story, have kids discuss the following questions in their groups:

● **What risks were involved for the main character?**

● **How will (or did) the main character receive a reward for taking the risk?**

● **What could you do this week to live out your faith in a similar way?**

After the last story has been discussed, say: **It sounds much more exciting to take life-and-death risks like Rahab's than to take the everyday risks of living like Christians. Yet, our everyday risks can seem so real, and the rewards can seem so uncertain. But when you trust God, the rewards outweigh the risks.**

4. What's the Question?

(You'll need 3×5 cards, pencils, and Bibles.)

Have everyone find a new partner to form pairs. Make sure each pair has a Bible, two 3×5 cards, and pencils.

Say: **Sometimes, stories about Bible heroes raise questions in our minds. For example, with the story of Rahab and the spies in the book of Joshua, we might ask questions like "Was it OK for Rahab to lie?" or "Why would God use a prostitute to help the Israelites?"**

Well, now's your chance to ask questions about this story. With your partner, read Joshua 2:1-15, 18 and 6:16-17 again, then come up with two questions you'd like to ask about this story. Write each question on a separate 3×5 card. You've got five minutes. Go.

After five minutes, collect kids' questions and mix them up in a stack.

Ask for a volunteer to come forward and pick one question out of the stack. Then read the chosen question aloud and give pairs 60 seconds to brainstorm their answers to the question. Allow a few pairs to report their answers to the class, then repeat the process for as long as time allows.

Afterward, say: **Sometimes you'll have questions about what you should or shouldn't do, but you can be certain of one thing: When you trust God, the rewards outweigh the risks.**

5. Spies and Soldiers

Say: **The soldiers believed Rahab's story and looked for the spies outside the city gate. Rahab and the spies were in a race for their lives. The soldiers wanted to "freeze" Israel's advance. In the game we're going to play, half of you will be soldiers and the other half, spies. One person needs to play the part of Rahab.**

Designate one person to act as Rahab. Form the rest of the class into two equal teams, the soldiers and the spies. Have the teams clear all tables and chairs away from the center of the room. Then have the spies stand at one end of the room and the soldiers stand in the middle of the room.

Say: **If you're a spy, your goal is to make it to the other end of the playing area. If you're a soldier, your goal is to "freeze" the spies by tagging them before they get across the room. Rahab can "unfreeze" a spy by tapping him or her.** If your classroom is small, you can make the game safer by having everyone hop on one foot.

Let the kids play until one team is ahead or wins conclusively. Then have everyone form a circle. Ask volunteers to respond to these questions:

● **What emotions did you have when you were trying to escape being tagged? When you were trying to tag someone?**

● **How were your emotions like the emotions you feel when you take risks in real life?**

● **What things "freeze" you and keep you from taking risks?**

● **How can trusting God "unfreeze" you to take risks for God?**

● **What is one risk you want the courage to take this week?**

Say: **Some people live their whole lives as if they are frozen. But when you trust God, you can dare to take risks. When you trust God, the rewards outweigh the risks.**

6. Red Ribbons

(You'll need red ribbon, scissors, a table or chair, and a Bible.)

Say: **The spies gave Rahab a red cord to hang in her window. That was how she and her family were saved from the wreckage of Jericho. The wall fell down, but Rahab's family was saved. Each of you is going to get a red ribbon to** **remind you of the story and to remind you that when you trust God, the rewards outweigh the risks.**

While you hand out pieces of red ribbon, have kids choose a partner. Once everyone has a partner and a ribbon, say: **Take the ribbon and tie it around your partner's wrist. As you tie the ribbon, tell how your partner has shown that he or she trusts God. For example, you might say, "You always come to Sunday school and listen so closely. I can tell you're really interested in God."**

After everyone has had a chance to share and exchange ribbons, form a circle. Tie a 2-foot length of red ribbon around a Bible and set the Bible on a table or chair in the center of the circle. Say: **When you trust God, the rewards outweigh the risks because God is completely trustworthy.**

Close with a prayer thanking and affirming God for being trustworthy. One at a time, have kids come forward to tie a knot in the ribbon. As they tie the knot, have them say a single-sentence prayer like "I trust you, God" or "Thank you, God, for being trustworthy."

WHAT WOULD YOU DO?

Directions: Read the situations below and discuss in your group the questions that follow.

WHAT WOULD YOU DO?

Situation #1—Your friends are all at your house talking. Your mom walks in and asks you to do one of your chores that you forgot to do that morning. What would you do? How would you feel?

WHAT WOULD YOU DO?

Situation #4—Your Sunday school teacher wants volunteers to talk during a worship service about what faith in Jesus means. Everyone is too scared to do it. What would you do? What would you say if you volunteered to speak?

WHAT WOULD YOU DO?

Situation #2—At school one of your friends makes fun of a guy in your class because his father is a minister. What would you do? How would that affect you and your friend?

WHAT WOULD YOU DO?

Situation #3—After your friend's father dies, you go and see your friend at the funeral home. She is really sad, and you want to help. While you are talking to her, some of the really "cool" girls from school come in. What would you do? With whom would you spend time? How could the decision change your relationship with your friend? with the "cool" girls?

WHAT WOULD YOU DO?

Situation #5—The person who sits next to you in class doesn't know the answer to one of the questions on a surprise quiz. What would you do? Would it make a difference if the person were your best friend? What could happen to you if you didn't help? What could happen to you if you did help?

Permission to photocopy this handout from *Fun-to-Learn Bible Lessons: Grades 4 & Up* granted for local church use. Copyright © Group Publishing, Inc., Box 481, Loveland, CO 80539.

7. God's X-Ray Vision (Samuel)

Kids definitely feel judged according to their physical appearance. If they have a "bad-hair day," it can mean disaster for family and friends. God, thankfully, judges us by his own standards. He doesn't judge us by what's on the outside, but by what's within. Use this lesson to help your students understand that God sees who they are on the inside.

A POWERFUL POINT

God sees who we are on the inside.

A LOOK AT THE LESSON

1. Mask It (7 minutes)
2. Bag It (10 minutes)
3. Campaign Posters (10 minutes)
4. Sticker Spots (10 minutes)
5. Blow It (7 minutes)
6. Royalty Rings (6 minutes)

THE FUN-TO-LEARN LESSON

1. Mask It

(You'll need paper plates, markers, scissors, tape, and string.)

As students arrive, point them to a table on which you have put paper plates, markers, scissors, tape, and string. Instruct each student to make a mask using the materials provided.

After everyone has arrived and completed a mask, have kids put on their masks. Have an impromptu "fashion show" by calling kids, one at a time, to the front of the room to model their masks. Encourage applause for each mask.

After all the kids have displayed their masks, have them take off their masks, choose partners, and discuss the following questions together.

● **What ideas did you have in mind as you were making your mask?**

● **What sorts of feelings does your partner's mask bring out in you?**

● **How would you react to a person who really looked like your mask? Explain.**

● **How important is a person's appearance to kids at your school? What aspects—like clothes or hair—affect how others think of a person?**

● **How important do you think a person's appearance is to God? What determines how God thinks of a person?**

Say: **The first thing we notice about someone is what he or she looks like. But God can see who we really are—not just what we look like. God sees who we are on the inside.**

2. Bag It

(You'll need paper grocery bags, a book, a rock, a feather, dirt, cotton balls, a one-dollar bill, gummy worms, paper, pencils, blindfolds, and Bibles.)

Say: **Let's see how good you are at figuring out what's on the inside.**

Set up eight paper grocery bags on a table. Place one of the following items in each bag: book, rock, feather, dirt, cotton balls, banana, one-dollar bill, and gummy worms. Do not label the bags and do not allow anyone to see the items in them.

Have kids form a line at one end of the table, then blindfold each student.

Say: **As you carefully make your way along the table, reach into each bag and touch the item that's in there. There are eight bags. Don't miss any. Don't tell anyone what you feel, but try to identify each item and remember what it is. When you reach the end of the table, write down what you felt in each bag.**

Have blindfolded kids work their way along the table. As each student reaches the end, take off his or her blindfold, provide paper and a pencil, and have the student list the contents of the eight bags. When everyone is done, ask:

● **If you could pick one bag for yourself, which one would you choose? Explain.**

● **How many of the items can you name from the bags?** As kids read their lists aloud, reveal the contents of the bags.

Form groups of no more than three people. Have each group select a Scripture reader, a secretary, and a reporter.

Hand out Bibles and give each secretary a sheet of paper and a pencil. Have the readers read 1 Samuel 16:1-13 to their groups. Ask:

● **How was Samuel's job like your task with the bags?**

● **What made Samuel's job difficult?**

● **How would you have felt if you were one of David's brothers?**

● **How would you have felt if you were David?**

● **If Samuel were here now, would you be more comfortable with how you look on the outside or what you are like on the inside? Explain.**

● **How do you feel knowing that God looks at your heart?**

Say: **God sees who we are on the inside. God helped Samuel understand that it's not what's on the outside that's important—it's the heart that matters. But not everyone realizes that. Let's imagine how the people of Israel might have responded to Samuel's—and God's—choice of a king.**

3. Campaign Posters

(You'll need construction paper, markers, and Bibles.)

Have kids stay in their groups of three. Hand out construction paper and markers.

Say: **Not everyone would have picked David as king. Some people probably thought one of David's brothers would have been a more likely candidate. In your trio, make two campaign posters—one for David and one for the brother of your choice. Look at 1 Samuel 16:1-13 for the good qualities of your candidates, then play up those qualities on your posters.**

Allow three or four minutes for groups to work. Then have students number off within their groups from one to three. Say: **Discuss the next few questions in your groups. Then I'll call out a number from one to three. The person in your group whose number I call out will be responsible for sharing your answer.**

Ask:

● **Which candidate would you have campaigned for? Why?**

● **If kings had been elected by popular vote instead of by God's anointing, do you think David would have been elected? Why or why not?**

● **What external things, like appearance or belongings, are important for someone who is popular today?**

● **What internal things, like friendliness or kindness, are important for someone who is popular?**

● **What external things do you look for in a friend? What internal things do you look for in a friend?**

● **Verse 17 says that God's Spirit worked in David. What is there about you that shows other people that God's Spirit is working in you?**

● **What could you do this week to let God's Spirit show more clearly in your life?**

Say: **God sees who we are on the inside. When we have Jesus in our hearts we change outwardly, too. Then other people can begin to see not just what we look like on the outside but what we're like on the inside as well.**

4. Sticker Spots

(You'll need stickers, chairs, a flash-light, and Bibles.)

Ask the class to clear away the tables and chairs from the center of the room. Then form a circle of chairs. Remove one chair from the circle and have one person stand in the center of the circle. Give each student 10 stickers.

Say: **For this activity, when I call out different parts of the body (for example, "elbow"), you must get out of your chair and put a sticker on someone's elbow, then quickly** find a different chair to sit in. You may not put a sticker on the person right next to you. If you're not quick, the person in the middle may steal your chair. If you lose your seat, you must stand in the middle and try to get a seat on the next round. The goal is to be seated and have no stickers left after 10 rounds.

Call out different parts of the body (such as elbow, wrist, ankle, foot, forehead, ear, shoulder, back, knee, and finger). After 10 calls, see how many kids got rid of all their stickers.

Put another chair in the circle and have everyone stand in front of a chair. Hand out Bibles to the kids who got rid of all their stickers and have them read Psalm 139:1-6 aloud together.

Give kids a few seconds to think after each of the following questions and tell them you'd like to hear lots of interesting responses. Have more stickers available, and when one student shares an answer, allow the other children who thought of the same answer and have nothing more to add to place a sticker on you. When everyone has "stickered" you, ask the next question and repeat the process. Ask:

● **What was it like to have people put stickers on you?**

● **Do you ever feel crowded or annoyed by people being too close to you or touching you? Tell about a situation that made you want more space.**

● **What kind of physical closeness did you like when you were a child?**

Read verse 5 aloud again. Ask:

● **How do you feel about the idea that God is all around you and that God's hand is on you?**

● **What are some ways that God might "put his hand on you"?**

Say: **God knows all about our bodies because God made our bodies. But God sees who we are on the inside, too.** Ask the person who was the last one standing in the game to read Psalm 139:23-24 out loud. Then ask:

● **What might make you nervous about having God examine your heart and thoughts? Explain.**

● **Why would anybody ask God to look inside them?**

● **How might God help you if you open your heart and thoughts to him?**

Say: **God sees who we are on the inside. Sometimes God sees bad things that keep us from being on the road to everlasting life (like verse 24 talks about). But God doesn't want to kick us off that road; God wants to lead us to everlasting life.**

Hold up a flashlight. Say: **Let's ask God to turn a spotlight on our hearts and show us what needs to change so we can stay on the right road.**

Pass the flashlight around the circle, having each person say a one-sentence prayer for God to examine his or her heart.

Say: **God sees who we are on the inside. In fact, God knows us better than we know ourselves. Let's take a moment to reflect on what God sees inside us. Please sit silently while we have a time for just you and God.**

Pause for about two minutes, then proceed to the next activity.

5. Blow It

(You'll need balloons, candy, pennies, and small paper wads.)

Say: **Let's explore more about how God sees who we are on the inside.**

Hand out the balloons in which you have put a small piece of candy, a penny, or a paper wad. Have the kids blow up their balloons.

Say: **You have one minute to trade balloons. Be careful and don't let your balloons burst. After one minute, I'll give the signal and you can pop your balloons to see what's inside.**

Let kids trade balloons for one minute, then call time. Signal for kids to burst their balloons. Then form a circle and ask:

● **Everyone who has a birthday in the winter, what was going through your mind when you were trading balloons?**

● **Everyone born in the spring, what did you think was in the different balloons you handled? How did that influence your trading?**

Teacher Tip

For the sake of this debriefing, define the seasons as follows:

Winter: December, January, and February.

Spring: March, April, and May.

Summer: June, July, and August.

Fall: September, October, and November.

● **Everyone born in the summer, how do you feel about what you finally got?**

● **Everyone born in the fall, how was judging these balloons from the outside like judging people from the outside?**

● **Everyone born in the winter, how would the trading have been different if all the balloons were clear?**

● **God sees what we're like on the inside just as easily as we could see through a clear balloon.**

Everyone born in the spring, what are some "paper wads" God might see in your life?

● Everyone born in the summer, what good things does God see in you?

● Everyone born in the fall, what other good qualities would you like to develop?

Say: **It was obvious what was inside some of the balloons. Others weren't quite so easy. It wasn't easy to know what the paper wads might have been. They could have been dollar bills! But you didn't know until we could see inside. You meet so many different people every day. And they all look so different. You can't be sure what's inside them, can you? We can only see on the outside. But God sees who we are on the inside. Some of the most unlikely people have greatness in them. We just need to give them a chance. God can make anyone great if he lives in your heart.**

Hand out candy to those kids who didn't get any in the balloons.

6. *Royalty Rings*

(You'll need a ring, a pad of 1×3 Post-It notes, pencils, and Bibles.)

Form a circle. Hand out Bibles and have the group read 1 Peter 2:9 aloud together.

Hold up a ring and say: **According**

to 1 Peter 2:9, we are royalty if we belong to Jesus. When you become a Christian, your heart is made clean and new. We are like kings and queens in training.

All of us have royal characteristics like kindness, fairness, caring, giving, love for God, humility, gentleness, leadership ability, and a willingness to help others. Let's think about the characteristics that are found on the inside, not the outside.

Have kids return to the groups of no more than three that they used in the "Bag It" and "Campaign Posters" activities and sit in circles on the floor. Give each trio three blank Post-It notes and pencils.

Say: **In Bible history, a special ring was a sign of royalty. Right now, think of one "royal" characteristic about the partner to your right and write it on your Post-It note. Then wrap the Post-It note around your partner's finger to create a "ring of royalty." Tell that partner why you chose that word to describe him or her.**

When partners are finished, wrap up the lesson by saying: **God sees who we are on the inside. This week, let's all try to look past external characteristics and see who people really are—on the inside.**

8. The Great Request (Solomon)

God told Solomon he would grant Solomon whatever he asked for. Solomon asked for wisdom to rule God's people. His unselfish answer so pleased God that God gave Solomon much more than he asked for—including wealth, fame, and peace.

"Look out for #1!" "If it feels good, do it!" These phrases bombard our society today. But God's way for our lives is much different. Use this lesson to teach your students what Jesus meant when he said to "lay down our lives" and to understand the effects on ourselves and others in doing so.

A POWERFUL POINT

Being unselfish brings joy to us, others, and God.

A LOOK AT THE LESSON

1. I Wish... (7 minutes)
2. Wise Guy (10 minutes)
3. Look Out for #1! (10 minutes)
4. Time Travelers (15 minutes)
5. Pray for One Another (4 minutes)
6. Unselfishness Brings Joy (4 minutes)

THE FUN-TO-LEARN LESSON

1. I Wish . . .

Say: **Let's pretend I have the power to grant you one request. You can have anything in the world you want. You have three minutes to find a partner and take turns discussing the one thing you would ask for and why.**

After about three minutes, ask pairs to discuss these questions:
- **What would your request be?**
- **Who would benefit from your request?**
- **How do you think God would feel about your request? Explain.**
- **If I told you your request had to be an unselfish request, how would your wish measure up?**

Allow several pairs to share the results of their discussions. Then say: **Being unselfish brings joy to us, others, and God. In our Bible story today God gave Solomon the chance to have whatever he asked for. Let's take a look at that story now.**

2. Wise Guy

(You'll need paper, pencils, newsprint, a marker, and Bibles.)

Form groups of four. Give each group Bibles, a sheet of paper, and a pencil. In each group have the kids appoint a reader who reads the Scripture, a recorder who writes down the group's answers, an encourager who urges everyone to participate, and a reporter who will share the group's answers with the rest of the class.

Have the reader read 1 Kings 3:4-15 to their groups. Then ask groups to discuss their answers to the following questions. Write the questions on newsprint for kids to refer to during discussions. Ask:

● **How would you have felt if God offered you anything you wanted?**

● **What would you have asked for?**

● **Do you think Solomon's choice was a good choice? Why or why not?**

● **Why do you think Solomon asked for wisdom?**

● **Why do you think God gave Solomon even more than he asked for?**

● **Why do you think Solomon's request for wisdom pleased God?**

● **If Solomon's request had been a purely selfish one, do you think God would have answered his request? Why or why not?**

When all the groups have finished, have reporters share their answers with the rest of the class. Then ask:

● **Solomon told God he felt like a child. Why do you think Solomon felt this way?**

Say: **Solomon had no knowledge of how to rule a kingdom. He asked the King of the world to give him wisdom to rule. He didn't want to make decisions or rules that would hurt or ruin people's lives. God was so pleased with this unselfish request that he rewarded Solomon greatly. Being unselfish brings joy to us, others, and God.**

3. Look Out for #1!

(You'll need name tags, pens, and Bibles.)

Say: **There is a very selfish phrase that we often hear repeated in our world today: "Look out for #1!"**

Ask:

● **What do you think this phrase means?**

● **How do you see this phrase in action in our society?**

Say: **Let's take a look at this phrase and see what we can do to change its meaning.**

Have a volunteer read Matthew 6:33. Ask:

● **As Christians, who is to have first place in our lives?**

● **How do we place God and his kingdom first in our lives?**

Form trios. Hand out name tags and pens. Ask each trio to make up a slogan that will help them remember to put God first. Have the kids write their phrase or slogan on name tags and attach the name tags to their clothing.

Allow kids to share their slogans with the rest of the class. After each slogan is presented, have kids discuss the following questions in their trios:

● **How could you live out this slogan this week?**

● **How would living out this slogan affect you?**

● **How would your living out this slogan affect people around you?**

Say: **When we put God first, we want to do what pleases him. Unselfishness brings joy to us, others, and God. So the next time you hear your slogan or the phrase "Look out for #1!" think about what would please God. He's #1 in your life.**

4. Time Travelers

(You'll need Bibles.)

Re-form the pairs you used in the "I Wish..." activity and have partners sit side by side facing you.

Say: **You have now become time**

machines. **Designate one person in your pair to be a forward controller and one to be a reverse controller.** (Pause.)

Now, think about the wish you shared with your partner at the start of our class. Imagine you actually received your request. Forward controller, lean forward to "move" your pair ahead in time to this day next year. Discuss these questions with your partner.

Ask:

● **How has the object or item you asked for affected you?**

● **How has it affected those around you?**

● **How has it made a positive impact on your life or another person's life?**

Say: **Now, reverse controller, lean backward to return your pair to the beginning of this class.** (Pause.)

Let's pretend I have the power to grant you one request. You can have anything in the world you want. You have three minutes to discuss with your partner the one thing you would ask for and why. You may change your request from the request you made earlier, if you like, or keep the same request.

Give kids a moment or two to discuss whether or not they'd change their requests. Then say: **Forward controller, lean forward to return your pair to the present.**

Ask:

● **Did you change your request? Why or why not?**

● **If Solomon had asked to be the wealthiest man in the world instead of asking for wisdom to rule, what do you think would have happened to his kingdom?**

● **When all we think about is ourselves, what we want, and how**

we feel, how does that affect those around us?

Hand out Bibles and have everyone read Matthew 23:11-12 in unison. Then have kids discuss the following questions with their partners:

● **How does selfishness prevent someone from being a servant?**

● **What happens to people who care only about themselves?**

● **How do we become great in God's sight?**

● **Describe a time when you were unselfish. Although it might have been hard to do, how did it make you feel inside?**

Have partners take turns reporting to the class one insight they've gained from the time-travel discussions.

Then say: **Being unselfish brings joy to us, others, and God. Because of Solomon's unselfishness, God gave him great rewards, and he became a great man. God exalted him. When we humble ourselves and become a servant to others, God will reward us, too.**

5. Pray for One Another

(You'll need paper and pencils.)

Give each person a piece of paper and a pencil.

Have kids tell their partners one unselfish thing they'll do this week, such as doing chores for a sibling or giving that sibling morning bathroom privileges first. Then tell kids to write down their partner's phone number so they can call their partner during the week to remind them to do this task.

Next, have kids spend 60 seconds in silent prayer for each other, asking God to give their partners strength to die to selfishness.

6. Unselfishness Brings Joy

(You'll need Almond Joy candy bars.)

Say: **Being unselfish brings joy to us, others, and God. God will reward you for your unselfishness this week, but I'd like everyone to have a small reward before leaving class. And I'm going to give you a chance to practice being unselfish!**

I'm going to give you each a candy bar. But if you're really committed to being unselfish this week, you'll give your candy bar to your partner. As you do, tell your partner one thing you've seen that person do that shows unselfishness. For example, you might say, "You were unselfish when you listened to my ideas instead of doing all the talking yourself."

Give students each an Almond Joy candy bar and let them give their candy bar to their partners.

Say: **Being unselfish brings joy to us, others, and God. Share your Almond Joy candy bar with someone this week and enjoy it together!**

9. It's Show Time!
(Elijah)

God wanted to prove he was the one and only true God. To accomplish this, God chose Elijah to instigate a contest between Baal and God. Elijah did what God told him to do and then depended completely on God to manifest his power.

Dependence upon God is an ongoing process. The more we know about God, the more we know we can depend on him. In this lesson, kids will learn how and why they can depend on God in their everyday lives.

A POWERFUL POINT

We can depend on God.

A LOOK AT THE LESSON

1. Lean on Me (5 minutes)
2. Baal Bailed Out (15 minutes)
3. Altar Building (7 minutes)
4. Learning to Lean (10 minutes)
5. Day-to-Day Dependence (8 minutes)
6. A Time to Remember (10 minutes)

THE FUN-TO-LEARN LESSON

1. Lean on Me

Say: **Today we'll be talking about how we can depend on God. Let's start off with an activity to help us get a picture of what it means to depend on God.**

Have kids number off, alternating "one" and "two." Pair up each one with a two of similar physical size.

Have the ones pretend to be mimes and act as if they are leaning on something when actually they are not. Tell the ones to freeze, then ask the twos to look at their leaning classmates. After a moment or two, have the ones and twos exchange places.

Tell the twos to unfreeze and stand about a foot behind the ones with their palms flat on their partners' backs. Ask the ones to start leaning backward while their partners slowly shuffle back until the ones are totally leaning on the hands of their partners. (If kids find it hard to hold up the leaning person, put two pairs together and have three students support the leaning person's upper back and shoulders.) Give the kids a chance to switch positions.

Have kids discuss the following questions with their partners:

- **What is the difference between the first leaning activity and the second leaning activity?**
- **How did it feel trusting someone not to drop you?**
- **What would someone have to do to knock over the leaning person in the second activity?**
- **Of the two leaning activities, which one best illustrates dependence on God? Why?**
- **Why do you think God wants us to depend on him so completely?**

Say: **We can depend on God. If we are leaning completely on him, he won't let us fall. No one can push God around! In our Bible story today, King Ahab and his wife, Jezebel, tried to push around some of God's people, including Elijah. Elijah found himself in a situation where he knew he had to depend completely on God. Let's find out what happened.**

2. Baal Bailed Out

(You'll need photocopies of the "Questions for Sports Commentators" handout on pages 51 and 52, paper, and Bibles.)

Say: **Elijah was a prophet of God. King Ahab and his wife, Jezebel, worshiped idols. Jezebel hated God and had commanded all God's prophets to be destroyed. But Elijah and about 100 other prophets of God escaped and hid in caves.**

One day Elijah fearlessly came to Ahab and told him he wanted a contest between God and Ahab's false god, Baal. The people of Israel were trying to worship both God and Baal, and Elijah wanted them to know who the true God was. Elijah told Ahab to gather all of Israel at Mount Carmel along with the prophets of the false gods to witness a contest.

Let's imagine what this contest might've been like if it had been aired on national television.

Choose two or three outgoing kids to be sports commentators and one to play the part of Elijah. The rest of the class can be divided in half to play the prophets of Baal and the people of Israel.

Send the sports commentators to one corner of the room, Elijah and the people of Israel to another corner, and the prophets of Baal to a third corner. Ask the kids to take turns in their groups reading 1 Kings 18:20-40.

Give the "Questions for Sports Commentators" handout to the appropriate students to acquaint themselves with the questions and have them decide who will be in charge of which questions. Give the sports commentators rolled-up paper for microphones.

Tell the other groups to study the passage and try to anticipate what questions will be asked. Encourage them to explore how they think their characters would feel as the story unfolds.

When the kids are ready, have one of the sports commentators announce the contest in a lively manner like a television sports announcer would. Have the kids act out the story while the sports commentators take turns interviewing the different characters before, during, and after the contest.

During the contest, encourage the prophets to jump and yell around an imaginary altar. Prompt Elijah while he pantomimes his actions. Have the people of Israel sit and cheer the two contestants on. Make sure everyone listens while the sports commentators ask questions.

Ask one of the sports commentators to do a typical sign-off to end the show, then have everyone sit down.

Say: **You all did a great job! Everyone give yourselves a big pat on the back!**

Ask:

● **Tell me what you learned from this Bible story. What stood out to you the most?**

● **What emotions do you think Elijah felt during this contest? Why?**

Ask a volunteer to read 1 John 4:4.

● **Why do you think Elijah appeared to be so bold?**

Say: **God gave Elijah a great victory. We can depend on God because God has the power to make us victorious in any situation.**

3. Altar Building

(You'll need a table, a plastic plate, marshmallows, brown sugar, toothpicks, beef jerky, Kool-Aid, Red Hots candy, and Bibles.)

Gather kids around a table and say: **To help us remember Elijah's great victory, we're going to build a model of Elijah's altar.**

Place a plastic plate in the middle of the table within everyone's reach. Have kids number off from one to six. (If you have more than 24 students, divide the class in half and make two models.) Give kids the following supplies and assignments:

● Ones—Use 12 marshmallows as stones to build the altar.

● Twos—Use brown sugar to form a trench around the altar (much like a moat around a small sand castle).

● Threes—Lay toothpicks on top of the marshmallows.

● Fours—Tear beef jerky into pieces and place the pieces on top of the toothpicks.

● Fives—Pour Kool-Aid over the altar, filling the trench.

● Sixes—Sprinkle Red Hots on the altar to represent the fire of God.

When the model is completed, ask:

● **What do you think Elijah was thinking as he was making all these preparations?**

● **Why do you think Elijah poured water over the altar?**

● **Why do you think it took so long for God to answer Elijah's prayer?**

Ask a volunteer to read Elijah's prayer in 1 Kings 18:36. Ask another volunteer to read 1 John 5:14.

Ask:

● **Do you think Elijah really believed God would answer his prayer? Explain.**

● **When do you have trouble being sure God will answer your prayers?**

● **How do we know God will hear our prayers?**

Say: **The Bible says that God told Elijah to do everything he did. Elijah obeyed God and depended on God to answer his prayer. We can depend on God to answer our prayers when we know they agree with God's will.**

4. Learning to Lean

(You'll need construction paper, plain paper, scissors, pens, staplers, newsprint, a marker, and Bibles.)

Hand out Bibles, construction paper, plain white paper, scissors, pens, and staplers. List the following references on the newsprint:

● Psalm 91:9
● Psalm 106:1
● Luke 1:37
● Acts 10:34
● Hebrews 6:18
● 1 John 5:4

Show kids how to make an eight-page booklet by cutting two sheets of white paper in half, placing the four half-sheets inside a folded sheet of construction paper, and stapling through all the sheets along the folded edge.

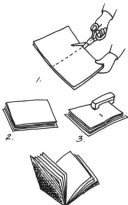

Point to the verse references you have posted and say: **Look up these verses and copy them into your booklet, one verse at the top of each page. Leave room on every page to write. If you write on the front and back sides of each page, you'll have two blank sides you can fill in with verses of your own choosing later.**

When everyone has completed a booklet, have them stand. Say: **Raise your hand when you've thought of an answer to the next question. I'd like to hear lots of different, interesting answers. When you've given an answer, you may sit down. If someone gives an answer you've thought of and you don't have anything more to add, you may sit down, too.**

Ask:

● **Which of these verses encourages you the most to depend on God? Explain.**

● **How could you use one of these verses this week?**

● **What other characteristics do you know about God that would help you to depend on him?**

Say: **The Bible tells us to depend on God. When we depend on God, we can be sure he will help and** encourage us. **Let's think about how we can depend on God in everyday events.**

5. Day-to-Day Dependence

Form two groups. Have one group form a circle inside the other circle and have kids face each other.

Say: **We can depend on God every day. I'm going to state a circumstance that would provide an opportunity to depend on God. For instance, let's say you need an outfit for a special occasion. You could depend on God to help you find something you like but can also afford. You could depend on God that no one else will buy the same outfit. You could depend on God to help you have a good time even if you can't get exactly the outfit you'd like.**

As I read each circumstance, think of a specific way you could depend on God in that situation, then relate it to the person standing in front of you. For the next circumstance, move one step to the right so you're facing a different person.

You may use these examples or make up your own.

● When taking a test
● When riding in a vehicle
● When eating food
● When riding your bike
● When playing a sport
● When you are sick
● When starting a new school year
● When moving to a new neighborhood

Say: **We can depend on God. He helps us in both the big things and the little things. Let's take a few minutes to share some ways God has helped us when we've depended on him.**

6. A Time to Remember

(You'll need the booklets from the "Learning to Lean" activity, pencils, and Bibles.)

Form pairs and say: **Take a few minutes and share with your partner a time when you depended on God for his help and God revealed his power. It can be as simple as the things we have just discussed or something bigger.**

After the kids have finished sharing, hand out pencils. Say: **Now trade booklets with your partner. On one of the pages, write your partner a brief note affirming the way your partner has depended on God in the past and encouraging your partner to depend on God in the future. For example, if your partner just shared about trusting God for help with a test, you could write, "You depended on God to get you through a tough test. You can depend on God to get you through anything!"**

Allow partners a few minutes to write in each others' booklets, then have partners take their own booklets back. Tell kids to write a prayer in their own booklets thanking God that he helps those who depend on him. For example, kids might write, "Thank you, Father, that nothing is impossible with you, and I can depend on you to help me make new friends."

When the kids are finished writing, have them look up Psalm 105:5 and read it silently. Ask:

● **Why do you think God wants us to remember his wonderful works?**

Ask kids to write the first phrase of Psalm 105:5 on the front cover of their booklets and to draw a picture of the altar model underneath.

Say: **When we remember what God has done, we know we can continue to depend on him. One of the reasons the Bible was written is so we can see how God worked in the lives of those who depended on him. As we read these stories, we can know he will do the same for us.**

Take your booklets home and start recording the times when you see God working in your life. Keep adding pages as you need them. When you get older you'll have a whole book to share with others about the wondrous works of God. Perhaps it might cause others to learn they can depend on God, too.

Encourage kids to bring their booklets back next week and share what they have written.

Questions for Sports Commentators

PART ONE

QUESTIONS BEFORE THE CONTEST

For the Prophets:

- Explain to our viewers the rules of this contest.
- Tell the viewers what your strategy is going to be.
- Do you think your god is going to win?
- How long do you think it will take before your god answers you?

For Elijah:

- Why did you call for this contest?
- What do you think will be the outcome? Why?

For the People:

- It's been reported that you don't know which is the real God, so you have been trying to worship both. Who do you think will be the victor in this contest? Why?

PART TWO

QUESTIONS DURING THE CONTEST

For the Prophets:

- We've been standing out here quite awhile. How are you guys feeling?
- What seems to be the problem?
- I heard Elijah say your god may be busy or sleeping. What do you think?

For Elijah:

- I keep hearing you make fun of this god, Baal, that the prophets worship. Why aren't you afraid of their god?
- We've been out here all day and it looks like the prophets have given up. What do you think your chances will be for your God to hear you? Why?

Questions for Sports Commentators

● It's your turn next. I'd like for you to tell our viewers exactly what your plans are.

For the People:

● We've been out here for quite some time now, and Baal still hasn't answered. Do you think he's going to? Why or why not?
● We just saw Elijah pour water over the altar. We know that water quenches fire. Do you think there is any possibility this God of his is that powerful? Explain.

PART THREE

QUESTIONS AFTER THE CONTEST

For the Prophets:

● Why don't you think you won this contest?
● I don't believe you guys have much of a future. Any last words?

For Elijah:

● Wow, it really wasn't much of a contest! Did you have any doubts that your God would prove himself?
● I noticed you specifically chose 12 stones with which to build the altar. Why did you do that?
● Tell our viewers what you think would have happened to you if your God hadn't sent the fire.

For the People:

● How did you feel when you saw fire fall that was hot enough to even dry the water in the ditch?
● What do you feel about Elijah's God now?
● What do you think should happen to the prophets of Baal?

Permission to photocopy this handout from *Fun-to-Learn Bible Lessons: Grades 4 & Up* granted for local church use. Copyright © Group Publishing, Inc., Box 481, Loveland, CO 80539.

10. My Shepherd (Psalm 23)

Psalm 23 is a favorite of many. The beautiful picture of God as our loving shepherd who gives, comforts, guides, and rewards is as relevant today as it was when it was written thousands of years ago. In this lesson, you'll walk kids through Psalm 23 verse by verse to help them realize that no matter how desolate or dangerous this world may seem, God provides for them and protects them.

A POWERFUL POINT

God provides for us and protects us.

A LOOK AT THE LESSON

1. Bumper Sticker Slogans (7 minutes)
2. Having It All (13 minutes)
3. Rest Stop (7 minutes)
4. Tread Rightly (10 minutes)
5. Are You Ready for Some Real Food? (12 minutes)
6. It's a Wonderful Life (6 minutes)
7. Thanks a Mint! (5 minutes)

THE FUN-TO-LEARN LESSON

1. Bumper Sticker Slogans

(You'll need construction paper, scissors, markers, and newsprint.)

Form pairs. Hand out construction paper, scissors, and markers.

Say: **Work with your partner to write a bumper sticker slogan comparing God with a familiar product or object. For example, God is like Coca-Cola: He's the real thing; God is like Hallmark greeting cards: He cares enough to send the very best; or God is like a flashlight: He lights my way. Cut paper into an appropriate size and shape for your bumper sticker, then write your slogan on it.**

After about three minutes, have kids display their bumper stickers. Then have kids discuss the following questions with their partners:

● **What qualities of God did these bumper stickers make you think of?**

● **How do comparisons like these help you understand what God is like?**

On a sheet of newsprint write, "God is like a shepherd: He provides for us and protects us."

Say: **Psalm 23 compares God with a shepherd and compares us with God's sheep.**

Ask:

● **What do you know about shepherds?**

● **What do you know about sheep?**

● **In what ways do you think God is like a shepherd?**

● **In what ways do you think you are like a sheep?**

Say: **Like a good shepherd cares for his sheep, God provides for and protects us. Let's take a closer look at how God gives us what we need.**

Teacher Tip

Here is some information about shepherds and sheep that may help you spark discussion if kids seem unfamiliar with the analogy of Psalm 23.

In Bible history, *shepherds* were the image of a caring protector. A good shepherd knew how many sheep were in his flock and could call each sheep by name. In addition, the shepherd of Bible history provided for all the needs of his flock—even risking his own life to protect the sheep from the dangers of wild animals.

The image of *sheep* presented in Bible history is one of an animal totally dependent on its shepherd for food, water, and protection from harm. A flock of sheep required constant care—being tended day and night by the shepherd. And sheep were known to recognize their shepherd's voice and follow.

---

2. Having It All

(You'll need poster board, old magazines, scissors, glue, paper, pencils, and Bibles.)

Form two teams. Give each team a poster board, several magazines, scissors, and glue. Ask a volunteer to read aloud Psalm 23:1.

Say: **You have four minutes to look through the magazines, cut out pictures of things people need, and glue them to the poster board. Everyone must cut out at least one picture. It's OK if different people find the same things. Try to cover the entire poster board with pictures.**

Let kids work on their posters for four minutes. Then call time and have teams take turns displaying their posters. Ask each person to identify which picture(s) he or she cut out. Give each team a sheet of paper and a pencil and have teams turn their poster boards over.

Say: **Choose one person from your team to write. When I say "go," you'll have two minutes to tell your writer as many items as you can remember from the other team's poster. The writer will write the items on the back of your poster. If there was more than one of an item, record how many there were.**

Give kids the signal to begin and let them work for two minutes. Then call time and compare each team's list with the other team's poster.

Take a few minutes to compare and declare a team winner. Then have the two teams form two lines facing each other.

Say: **The person facing you in the other line is now your partner. Discuss my first question with him or her. Then rotate one position to the left for a new partner and answer my next question. If you're at the left end of the line when it's time to rotate, simply move around to the other end. Keep rotating and answering each new question with a new partner.**

Ask:

● **How did you feel when you were trying to remember the pictures on the other team's poster?**

● **Which of the things pictured do you most often take for granted?**

Say: **Sometimes it's hard for us to remember that God is the one who supplies all of our needs. When your parents buy food and clothing, God is the one who gives the resources to buy those things. When you wake up each morning and take that first breath, it is God who has supplied the air. These are things we shouldn't take for granted, and we should remember to thank God for them.**

Hand out Bibles. Ask all the kids in

one line to read aloud Philippians 4:19 together. Then ask:

● **What are some intangible (nonphysical) needs people have, such as love and security?**

● **How can God meet those intangible needs in ways that no one else can?**

● **What intangible needs do you want God to meet this week?**

Say: **God provides for and protects us. God gives us both the physical and intangible things we need. Let's think about some of the intangible needs God provides for us.**

3. Rest Stop

(You'll need hymn books and Bibles.)

Give each child two hymn books. Tell the kids to put one hymn book on each hand and stretch both arms out to their sides. Have them walk around in this position for 60 to 90 seconds without bending their elbows. Ask the kids to return the books to you, then lie on their backs on the floor.

Say: **While you're lying on the floor, close your eyes and think about yourself in a meadow of green grass with the wind gently blowing. Then raise your hand when you've thought of an answer to the next question. I'd like to hear lots of different, interesting answers. When you've given an answer, you may roll over and lie on your stomach. If someone gives an answer you've thought of and you don't have anything more to add, you may roll over, too.**

Ask:

● **What went through your mind when you carried the hymn books?**

● **How did it feel to drop your arms?**

● **How would you feel about me if I had forced you to do this exercise for about five minutes without resting?**

● **What does rest do for our bodies?**

● **What would happen if you never got to rest?**

Read Psalm 23:2-3a.

● **Why would a good shepherd make sure his sheep got to rest?**

● **How does God give us rest?** (If kids don't suggest it themselves, ask them to consider emotional and mental rest as well as physical rest.)

● **What are some ways that people resist taking a rest?**

● **When do you think you'll need a rest or a break—either physically, mentally, or emotionally—this week?**

● **How does it make you feel to know that God knows when you need a break and wants to give you a break?**

Say: **Sometimes we get physically, mentally, or emotionally tired. God provides for and protects our bodies by giving us rest so we can continue to work or think or whatever we need to do. Let's discover what else is in Psalm 23.**

4. Tread Rightly

(You'll need photocopies of the "A Course, of Course" handout on page 59, scissors, paper, pencils, tape, and Bibles.)

Form two groups, group 1 and group 2. Have each group go to opposite ends of the room. Cut apart a copy of the "A Course, of Course" handout.

Give each group its directions from the handout, scissors, paper, pencils, and tape.

Say: **Following the directions on the handout I gave you, lay out a** course for the other team to follow. **If you have trouble thinking of ideas, read Galatians 5:19-23.**

Have the teams work on their courses. When both groups are finished, have each group designate a leader.

Have the leader of group 1 lead that group through the obstacle course that group 2 set up, reading aloud the signs and directions.

Have the members of group 2 form a line with each person holding onto the waist of the person in front. Have the leader of group 2 lead the group along the footprint path without walking on any negative trait.

When the kids reach the end of each course, have group 1 form a circle facing outward. Have group 2 form a circle around group 1, facing inward, so that kids are facing each other. Say: **The person facing you is now your partner. Discuss my first question with him or her, then move to the right to get a new partner for the next question.**

Ask:

● **How did your leader help you?**

● **How did it feel knowing you had a designated leader and all you had to do was follow that leader?**

● **What might have happened if you hadn't followed your leader?**

Read Psalm 23:3b-4.

● **How does God lead us? What resources does God use?**

● **Why do you think God wants to lead us on the right paths?**

● **How does this passage give you courage for the rough times in your life?**

● **What does God do for you during these hard times?**

Say: **God provides for and protects us. One way God does that is by leading us, even in rough times.**

5. Are You Ready for Some Real Food?

(You'll need Hershey's Kisses and Bibles.)

Read Psalm 23:5a. Say: **This verse talks about God preparing a meal for us. To understand what that verse means, let's do two experiments focusing on eating.**

Give each person two Hershey's Kisses.

Say: **Find a partner for these experiments. First, I want you to feed each other one of the Hershey's Kisses. Now, chew the Hershey's Kiss a couple of times, then quickly swallow it.** Pause while kids follow your directions. **Now feed your partner the other piece.** (Pause.) **Before you eat this time, suck on the Hershey's Kiss for a little bit before you chew it slowly. Savor the taste before swallowing.** Again wait while kids follow your directions.

After kids have fed each other the chocolate, give each pair a Bible.

Say: **For the second experiment, designate one person to read and one person to listen.** When each pair has chosen a reader, have the readers turn to Psalm 119:97-104.

Say to the readers: **Read Psalm 119:97-104 to your partner as fast as you can.** When the readers are done reading, say: **Now ask your partner a question about the passage.** Give kids a few moments to think of a question to ask.

Say: **It's OK if your partner didn't know the answer to your question because you're going to give your partner a second chance. Read the same passage over again slowly, then ask your partner another question.**

When all the pairs are finished,

have them switch roles and repeat the process with Psalm 19:7-11. Then have partners discuss the following questions:

Teacher Tip

You may not have time for kids to discuss all of the questions in this activity—that's OK. You may want to give pairs different questions to discuss or simply choose a few questions you think are most compelling for your kids and have pairs discuss those.

● **What did our experiment with the Hershey's Kisses and our experiment with the Bible passages have in common?**
● **What conclusions could you draw about either hurrying or taking your time with these experiments?**
● **How do you think the Bible is like food?**
● **Would you say you usually treat the Bible as a banquet to be savored or as fast food to be gulped? Explain.**
● **How would you benefit from "feeding" on God's Word?**
● **What could you do this week to feast on the Bible? Be specific.**

Say: **God provides for and protects us. God not only gives us the food our bodies need, God also gives us the Bible to help us grow and keep us safe from evil.**

6. It's a Wonderful Life

(You'll need construction paper, scissors, transparent tape, pencils, and Bibles.)

Hand out construction paper, scissors, and tape and have kids cut out crowns to fit their heads. When the

kids are finished, read Psalm 23:5b.

Say: **In Bible times, oil was poured on someone's head to show that God was pleased with that person. It would be like a king placing a crown on our heads and telling us that we could have anything he owned. In fact, God tells us we are his royal people.**

Seat kids in a circle and have them put on their crowns. Hand out Bibles and have everyone read 1 Peter 2:9 in unison. Then read Psalm 23:6 together.

Hand out pencils. Have kids pass their crowns around the circle and take turns writing on each crown one good thing that God gives us; for example, parents, friends, and the Bible. Encourage kids to think of different things for each crown. If you have time, let kids share what was written on their crowns.

Say: **God provides for and protects us. God has given us all the good things written on these crowns and more. One of the best things God has provided for us is heaven. Psalm 23 says we'll live in the house of the Lord forever. What a wonderful God we have!**

7. Thanks a Mint!

(You'll need individually wrapped chocolate mints such as York peppermint patties. You'll also need markers and Bibles.)

Give each child a wrapped chocolate mint and a marker. Ask the children to gently draw faces on their mint wrappers.

Say: **Psalm 23 talks about God as our shepherd and how God cares for us, his sheep. It talks about how God gives us what we need and how he loves and protects us. Your assignment this week is to** take care of this mint the way God takes care of us.

Ask: **What are some things you could do this week that would show you were a good shepherd over this mint? Some examples are to make sure the mint doesn't get eaten or stepped on; to take it with you wherever you go; and to never** let it out of your sight. Every time you look at your mint this week, remember that God provides for and protects us.

Close by having each person say a short prayer thanking God for a specific protection or provision, beginning with the phrase, "Thanks a mint, God, for..."

A Course, of Course

Directions: Photocopy and cut apart this handout for use during the "Tread Rightly" activity.

Group 1 ▼

Use your shoes to trace and cut out about 10 footprints. Brainstorm different positive and negative qualities, such as honesty and dishonesty, selfishness and unselfishness, and so on. Write one trait on each footprint. Tape the footprints on the floor to make a path across the room, intermixing the positive and negative qualities.

Group 2

Make an obstacle course using different objects found in the room. Each obstacle will represent a tough time or difficult situation someone might face in real life. Write on paper what each obstacle represents and how to conquer that obstacle. For instance, an overturned chair could be "A cliff of divorced parents. To conquer, crawl underneath." Torn pieces of paper could be "A sand trap of mean words. To conquer, tiptoe through them." Tape the paper to or beside each obstacle. Create four or five different obstacles and arrange them to make an obstacle course.

Permission to photocopy this handout from *Fun-to-Learn Bible Lessons: Grades 4 & Up* granted for local church use. Copyright © Group Publishing, Inc., Box 481, Loveland, CO 80539.

11. Vow Not to Bow (The Fiery Furnace)

King Nebuchadnezzar decreed that everyone was to bow down to his idol. Shadrach, Meshach, and Abednego followed God and refused to worship the king's statue. As a result, they were thrown into a blazing furnace. But God sent a visitor from heaven to protect them. When they came out, they didn't even smell like smoke! The God of Shadrach, Meshach, and Abednego was exalted!

Although few children will ever have to make a decision this life-threatening, they will inevitably find themselves in circumstances where they will be tempted to compromise their beliefs. Use this lesson to encourage your students to make a decision to live uncompromisingly in an increasingly compromising world.

A POWERFUL POINT

It takes courage to live for God.

A LOOK AT THE LESSON

1. What If . . . (8 minutes)
2. "Totally Cool" Museum (15 minutes)
3. On Fire for God (10 minutes)
4. Down on Your Knees (12 minutes)
5. Different Is Good (7 minutes)
6. Soar With the Spirit (5 minutes)
7. Just Do It! (3 minutes)

THE FUN-TO-LEARN LESSON

1. What If . . .

(You'll need photocopies of the "Questions?" handout on page 67, paper, pencils, and Bibles.)

Give each person one question from the "Questions?" handout, a sheet of paper, and a pencil.

Say: **On your blank sheet of paper write a possible outcome for the question on your slip of paper. For instance, if you have the question "What would happen if you heard a loud crash coming from your room?" you could write, "I would run to see what it was" or "I would sit and wonder what fell."**

Give kids a minute or two to write. When the kids are finished, have them sit in a circle. Tell them to pass their questions to the right and their answers to the left, checking to make sure that each person has a set of unmatched questions and answers. Then have kids read both aloud to the group, resulting in some funny combinations. If you have time, have the kids pass the papers on as before for new sets of questions and answers to be read.

Have kids stand as you ask the following questions. Give them a few seconds to think after each question and tell them you'd like to hear lots of interesting responses. When one student shares an answer, kids who thought of the same answer and have nothing more to add can sit down. When everyone is seated, ask the next question and repeat the process. (If all the kids sit down after the first student shares an answer, have kids stand up and ask the question again to encourage another response.)

Ask:

● **What made some of these question-and-answer combinations funny?**

● **Describe a time when you were in a situation that turned out worse than you thought it would.**

● **Describe a time when you were in a situation that turned out better than you thought it would.**

Read aloud Daniel 3:1, 4-6, and 8-27. Ask:

● **How do you think Shadrach, Meshach, and Abednego thought this situation would turn out?** If kids don't mention it, remind them that Shadrach, Meshach, and Abednego acknowledged the risk they were taking (verse 18).

● **Why do you suppose Shadrach, Meshach, and Abednego had the courage to take a stand for what they believed?**

● **In what situations do you need courage to live for God?**

Say: **It takes courage to live for God. Let's see what we can learn from Shadrach, Meshach, and Abednego about staying cool when the heat is on.**

2. "Totally Cool" Museum

(You'll need wrapping paper, scissors, transparent tape, rubber bands, a shoe box, drinking straws, pencils, an empty Cool Whip container, red streamers, an electric fan, and Bibles.)

Select two kids to form group 1. Divide the rest of the class in half to form group 2 and group 3.

Say: **Today we're going to create a museum of ancient artifacts. You are all archaeologists and have been digging in the ancient city of Babylon. In a moment, I'll assign you some Bible verses. Then, in your groups, read your assigned Bible verses and create the artifact or artifacts described in your particular passage.**

Tell group 1 to read Daniel 3:1-3 and make a statue. Provide gold wrapping paper, scissors, and tape. Tell the kids in group 1 that they may also use tables, chairs, and anything else in the room to build their statue.

Tell group 2 to read Daniel 3:4-18 and create musical instruments. Provide rubber bands, a shoe box, drinking straws, scissors, pencils, and a Cool Whip container. Encourage kids to use whatever other resources are in the room.

Tell group 3 to read Daniel 3:19-30 and construct a furnace. Provide red streamers, scissors, tape, and an electric fan. Have the kids section off a small corner of the room for their furnace. Then have them cut the red streamers into 1- to 2-foot sections and tape them to the boundaries of the furnace. When the fan is turned on, the streamers will blow around like fire.

Give kids a few minutes to work. If one group finishes before the others, ask that group to make up a name for the museum and create a poster to hang on the door.

When all the groups have completed their artifacts, say: **Select a spokesperson to be a "guide" for your area of the museum. Have the guide retell the story while the others in your group pantomime the actions from your Bible reading.**

Have groups perform in the order that their passages appear in the Bible.

If your class is small, kids from the other two groups may help pantomime while the guide speaks.

Afterward, form two lines facing each other. Say: **The person facing you in the other line is now your partner. Discuss my first question with him or her. Then rotate one position to the left for a new partner and answer my next question. If you're at the left end of the line when it's time to rotate, simply move around to the other end. Keep rotating and answering each new question with a new partner.**

Ask:

● **If there were a real museum featuring the artifacts from Shadrach, Meshach, and Abednego's experience, how big a tourist attraction do you think it would be? Explain.**

● **What makes Shadrach, Meshach, and Abednego worth remembering?**

● **If someone were to make a museum featuring your courage in living for God, what experience of yours could they include?**

● **Nebuchadnezzar would say the real hero of Shadrach, Meshach, and Abednego's museum is God.** Read aloud verse 28. **How clearly does your life point others to God?**

Say: **It takes courage to live for God. Standing up for what's right doesn't always guarantee a happy ending—at least not immediately. Let's take a look at the risks and rewards Shadrach, Meshach, and Abednego faced.**

3. On Fire for God

(You'll need Bibles.)

Form groups of four. Have students number off within their groups from one to four. Say: **Discuss the next few questions in your groups. Then I'll call out a number from one to four. The person in your group whose number I call out will be responsible for sharing your answer. Keep your Bibles open to Daniel 3 in case you want to refer back to the story during our discussion.**

Teacher Tip

Meaningful discussion takes time, particularly when kids get interested in a topic. There are probably more questions in this section than your groups will have time to answer—and that's OK. You know your group best, so feel free to pick and choose the questions you'll use during this activity. It's OK to skip some questions and spend more time on others.

Ask:

● **What would have been the best thing that could have happened to Shadrach, Meshach, and Abednego if they had bowed to the king's statue?**

● **What would have been some negative consequences for Shadrach, Meshach, and Abednego if they had bowed to the king's statue?**

● **Why do you think Shadrach, Meshach, and Abednego made the choice they did?**

● **If you had been in Shadrach, Meshach, and Abednego's situation, do you think you would have placed more importance on the immediate consequences of obeying God (getting thrown in the furnace) or the long-term consequences (pleasing God and receiving a reward in heaven if not on earth)? Explain.**

● **What would you think about this story if Shadrach, Meshach, and Abednego had died in the fur-**

nace? What would you think of their decision?

• **What situations do you face that require you to either compromise or take a stand for God?**

• **What are some risks in taking a stand for God?**

• **What are some rewards for taking a stand for God?**

• **What would you do if you weren't sure you'd get an immediate reward or "happy ending" in a particular situation?**

• **Describe a situation you might face this week that would challenge your courage to live for God. How might you handle that situation?**

Say: **It takes courage to live for God. You probably won't be threatened with a fiery furnace this week, but you *will* face other situations in which it would be easy to compromise. Let's look at some everyday situations that challenge our courage to stand up for what we believe.**

4. Down on Your Knees

(You'll need Bibles.)

Ask:

• **Do you think there were other people around Shadrach, Meshach, and Abednego who believed God but bowed down to the idol anyway? Explain.**

• **What are some things those people might have told themselves that would have made it easier for them to bow down?**

Say: **Let's take a closer look at how Christians today compromise or back down from what they believe in.**

Ask the kids to begin walking randomly around the room.

Say: **I'm going to read some situations. Each of the characters be-**

lieves in God, but they are placed in a situation where they must make a decision to do what God wants or back down from what they believe in. At the first sign of any compromise by the character, drop to your knees, lift your feet up, wrap your hands around your toes, and balance on your knees until I finish reading the situation. If the character stands fast in what he or she believes in, keep walking around and don't drop to your knees.

Read the following situations. After each, call on a few kids to explain how they think the character compromised or stood firm and what the character could have done differently.

Situation 1: **"Another pop quiz!" groaned Josh. He hadn't fared so well on the last one. The teacher began reading the questions, and Josh slowly wrote his answers.**

"I wonder if these answers are right?" he asked himself. "It wouldn't hurt to take a look at Alex's paper—just to compare answers. It wouldn't really be cheating," he reasoned.

Josh looked up to see if the teacher was looking and then glanced at Alex's paper.

•••

Situation 2: **The telephone rang. When Jody picked it up she immediately recognized the voice of her best friend, Anne.**

"Can I come over?" Anne asked breathlessly. "I just bought a new compact disk, and I want you to listen to it."

"No," Jody said dejectedly. "My parents just left for a teacher's meeting at church, and I'm not allowed to have anyone over."

"Oh, come on, Jody," whined Anne. "Your parents will never

know. I'll be gone before they get back."

"Well, if you're sure. Maybe it'd be OK as long as they didn't find out."

"OK, I'll be right over," Anne declared.

● ● ●

Situation 3: **Bryan was standing with his classmates waiting for the bus. As he listened to the differing conversations around him, it seemed everyone in the group had said, "Oh God!" at least once, and some had used other swear words as well. Bryan didn't want to swear, but he didn't want to be considered a goody-goody either. So when a classmate asked him what he thought of the social studies test, Bryan started his answer with, "Oh, Ga!" He reasoned that helped him fit right in, and that he wasn't technically swearing either.**

● ● ●

Situation 4: **Emily picked up a Snickers candy bar and gave her money to the clerk. The clerk quickly gave Emily her change and began checking out the next customer. As Emily walked toward the door, she realized the clerk had given her a quarter too much.**

"Oh, well," she said to herself, "it's only a quarter. Besides, I'm in a hurry, and the store will never miss a measly quarter anyway."

Emily began eating the candy bar as she walked out the door.

● ● ●

After kids have responded to all the situations, form two circles, one within the other. Have the members of the inner circle face outward and the members of the outer circle face inward so kids are facing each other.

Say: **The person facing you is now your partner. Discuss my first question with him or her, then move to the right to get a new partner for the next question.**

Ask:

● **What went through your mind as you listened to these situations?**

● **Which situations did you most relate to? Explain.**

Say: **Granted, these situations are not as serious or as life-threatening as Shadrach's, Meshach's, and Abednego's was, but let's take a look at how God feels about any type of compromising.**

Hand Bibles to the kids in the outer circle and have them read Romans 12:2 in unison. Ask:

● **How does this verse relate to the situations we discussed?**

● **How does this verse relate to your life?**

● **How do you feel about being different from the people around you?**

Say: **You might be thinking, "If I don't compromise, I'm really going to stand out!" Well, sometimes you will stand out. Shadrach, Meshach, and Abednego certainly did! It takes courage to live for God, especially when it calls for us to be different from our peers. Let's do an experiment to see what a difference being different can make!**

5. Different Is Good

(You'll need two balloons for each person—one should be filled with helium and have a string attached to it. You'll also need Bibles.)

Form pairs and have partners stand facing each other, about five feet apart. Give each child an uninflated balloon and have the kids blow up their balloons.

Say: **Bat your balloons back and forth to each other without catching them. Try to keep both balloons from hitting the ground. As soon as one balloon touches the ground, you and your partner must stop playing and sit down.**

When all play has stopped, give each child a helium-filled balloon. Tell them to do the very same activity. The balloons will float to the ceiling after the first bat. Then ask the pairs to get their Bibles and sit down.

Have one person in each pair read 1 Corinthians 6:19 aloud and the other read 2 Timothy 1:7. Then have the partners discuss the following questions together.

Ask:

● **How was the helium-filled balloon a good illustration of a person filled with the Holy Spirit?**

● **How does being filled with the Holy Spirit relate to having the courage to live for God?**

● **Do you feel more like an ordinary balloon or a helium-filled balloon? Explain.**

● **How can you have the power of the Holy Spirit in your life?**

● **What is one way you could act like a helium balloon instead of an ordinary balloon this week?**

Say: **It takes courage to live for God. Living for God means being different. But when you're filled with the Holy Spirit, different is good! Let's think about how we can soar with the Spirit!**

6. Soar With the Spirit

(You'll need the helium balloons from the "Different Is Good" activity, and markers.)

Have kids stand on chairs or tables to retrieve the balloons from the ceiling. When everyone has a balloon, hand out markers and have each person write his or her name on a balloon.

Next, say: **Let go of your balloon. Now grab the string of another balloon and see whose name is written on that balloon. Write a one-word description on the balloon of how that person can live when they're filled with the Holy Spirit. You might choose a word that reminds you of the story of Shadrach, Meshach, and Abednego, like "fearless" or "uncompromising." Or you might write another word that describes a characteristic of a person who allows God's Spirit to control his or her life, like "understanding" or "trustworthy."**

When kids have written on the balloons, have them release those balloons and find other balloons to write on. Warn them to handle the balloons carefully so the ink doesn't smear. Be sure to have a few extra balloons on hand in case some accidentally pop! Have kids try to write on every balloon.

When all the balloons have been written on, have kids find their own balloons and read what others wrote.

Say: **When the Holy Spirit helps you live for God, you're different from other people. It takes courage to be different. Do you have the courage to live for God?**

7. Just Do It!

Form a circle.

Say: **I'm going to give you a chance right now to make a decision that you will not compromise what you believe. It takes courage to live for God, but once you make that decision it will become easier to say no when faced with a compromising situation. Everyone close your eyes and silently make your commitment to God. As you do so, squeeze the hand of the person on your right. If your hand is squeezed, you need to pray sometime during this week for the person who squeezed your hand.**

Close in prayer thanking God that as Christians we are different and that this difference brings him glory.

Say: **Wow, our hearts feel light when we know we will not compromise our actions—almost as light as these balloons! Take your balloon home as a reminder of your commitment in class today.**

QUESTIONS

Directions: Photocopy and cut apart this handout for use in the "What If . . ." activity. Make enough copies for each student to have one question.

WHAT WOULD HAPPEN

if you heard a loud crash coming from your room?

WHAT WOULD HAPPEN

if a camera flashed in your face?

WHAT WOULD HAPPEN

if you brought home a bad report card?

WHAT WOULD HAPPEN

if you missed your school bus?

WHAT WOULD HAPPEN

if you had only three hours of sleep on a school night?

WHAT WOULD HAPPEN

if you put your shoes on the wrong feet?

WHAT WOULD HAPPEN

if you put three sticks of bubble gum in your mouth?

WHAT WOULD HAPPEN

if you tried to phone your friend and dialed a wrong number?

WHAT WOULD HAPPEN

if you ran outside in the rain without a coat?

WHAT WOULD HAPPEN

if you ate ice cream very fast?

Permission to photocopy this handout from *Fun-to-Learn Bible Lessons: Grades 4 & Up* granted for local church use. Copyright © Group Publishing, Inc., Box 481, Loveland, CO 80539.

12. Hope to the World, the Lord Is Come (Jesus' Birth)

Wouldn't it have been exciting to be present for Jesus' birth? Who wouldn't have felt a surge of hope hearing the angelic choir? But the excitement of the Nativity can seem far removed from your students when they face day-to-day disappointments and struggles in their own Christian growth. They need to discover for themselves that having a God who put on human flesh makes a difference to everyone in the human race—then and now. Use this lesson to help kids see that having a Savior who is both God and human is an awesome source of help and hope.

A POWERFUL POINT

Jesus' birth brought new hope for everyone.

A LOOK AT THE LESSON

1. Cupcake Creations (7 minutes)
2. A Hopeful Story (10 minutes)
3. Cross the Floor (9 minutes)
4. Growing Like Jesus (7 minutes)
5. Hope Ornaments (13 minutes)
6. Trimming the Tree (5 minutes)

THE FUN-TO-LEARN LESSON

1. Cupcake Creations

(You'll need plain, frosted cupcakes and a variety of cupcake toppings.)

Before class, set out a variety of cupcake toppings such as candy sprinkles, colored sugars, and small candies like gumdrops or chocolate chips. As students arrive, give each a plain, frosted cupcake. Let kids decorate their cupcakes with the toppings you've provided. Warn kids not to eat their cupcakes until you give the OK.

When everyone has decorated a cupcake, say: **Today we're going to talk about Jesus' birth. Our cupcakes will be the birthday treat. But first let's sing "Happy Birthday" to Jesus.**

Sing the song together, then let kids eat their cupcakes. When everyone is finished, have kids find partners and share their responses to the following questions:

● **What do you like best about birthday celebrations in your family?**

● **Which of your birthdays was the most memorable? Tell your partner a little about what made that birthday special.**

● **What hopes do you think your parents had for you when you were born?**

● **What hopes do you suppose Mary and Joseph had for Jesus when Jesus was born?**

● **What are some things you can dare hope for because of Jesus?**

Say: **Jesus' birth brought new hope for everyone. Let's take a look at what Jesus' birth meant to the people around Jesus.**

2. A Hopeful Story

(You'll need paper, pencils, and Bibles.)

Form three groups. Assign one group Luke 2:1-21, the second group Luke 2:22-38, and the third group Luke 2:39-52. Give each person a Bible, a piece of paper, and a pencil. Say: **Read your verses and answer my questions. Make sure everyone in your group writes down your group's answers because in a few minutes you will share your responses with people from the other groups.**

Ask:

● **How do you suppose the people in your passage (the shepherds, Simeon and Anna, or the teachers at the Temple) felt when they saw Jesus or heard about Jesus?**

● **What good things did the people in your passage hope Jesus would accomplish?**

● **If you had been one of the people in your passage, how might your life have been changed because of your encounter with Jesus?**

● **How can your life today be changed because of Jesus?**

When everyone has written down responses, say: **Now find new partners from the other two groups to form trios.** Have the kids read their passages aloud to their trios and share their responses. Then ask:

● **What do you think is the most exciting part of Luke 2? Why?**

● **What do you think is the most exciting part of being a Christian today?**

Say: **Jesus' birth brought new hope for everyone—not just for the people who lived in the time when Jesus was born, but for us today, too. Let's look at the hope we have because, in Jesus, God became human.**

3. Cross the Floor

(You'll need Bibles.)

Have everyone line up along the wall on one side of the room. Say: **The goal of this game is to get across the room. Follow my directions and see how far you get.**

Give directions like the following, adjusting as appropriate for your classroom's size:

● **If you did your best in school this week, take two steps forward.**

● **If you gave one of your family members a hug this morning, take two steps forward.**

● **If your mom or dad told you to do something this morning and you didn't do it, take two steps backward.**

● **If you did someone a favor without being asked this week, take two steps forward.**

● **If you have ever been mean to a friend, take two steps backward.**

Teacher Tip

If you have time, feel free to add more commands to this game; you're not limited to only the ones listed here.

It's not necessary to wait until someone makes it to the other end of the room—maybe no one will! After giving the commands, have students return to the side of the room where they started.

Say: **Raise your hand when you've thought of an answer to each of these questions. When you've given an answer, you may go stand on the other side of the room. If someone gives an answer you've thought of and you don't have anything more to add, you may go stand on the other side, too.** (If all the kids move across the room after the first student shares an answer, have kids go back, then ask the question again to encourage another response.)

Ask:

● **What went through your mind as I gave the directions in this game?**

● **How likely were you to make it all the way across the room? Explain.**

● **What did you learn about yourself as you responded to the directions?**

● **How was trying to make it across the room like trying to make it to heaven without Jesus' help?**

Hand out Bibles and have everyone read aloud Hebrews 4:14-16 together.

Ask:

● **What are some weaknesses you want Jesus to understand?**

● **How does it make you feel to know that Jesus faced the same problems and temptations you face?**

● **What hopes do you have because of these verses?**

● **What is one thing you want to ask Jesus to help you with this week?**

Say: **Jesus' birth brings us hope. Jesus not only has the awesome power of God, Jesus also understands what we are going through because he went through the same things himself—only without sinning.**

4. Growing Like Jesus

(You'll need Bibles.)

Say: **Jesus' birth brought new hope for everyone. Because Jesus became like us, we can become more and more like Jesus. Let's find out what Jesus was like when he was growing up.**

Have kids form pairs. Have the person in each pair wearing the most but-

tons join in unison with those from other pairs to read aloud Luke 2:52. Then ask pairs to discuss the following questions. Have partners take turns reporting their answers to the class before you ask each new question. Ask:

● **Luke 2:52 says that Jesus became wiser. What sorts of things show that God is helping someone grow mentally?**

● **Luke 2:52 says that Jesus grew physically. What sorts of things show that God is helping someone grow physically?**

● **Luke 2:52 says that people liked Jesus. What sorts of things show that God is helping someone be likable?**

● **Luke 2:52 says that God was pleased with Jesus. What sorts of things please God today?**

Say: **Now tell your partner some positive thing about his or her intelligence or physical abilities, something people like about your partner, or something about your partner that pleases God.**

Let kids choose which of these categories they want to affirm in their partners; if they are limited to one category they may have trouble thinking of something and end up hurting their partners' feelings.

Afterward say: **Jesus' birth brought new hope for everyone. Because Jesus was like us growing up, we can become more and more like Jesus.**

5. Hope Ornaments

(You'll need clear plastic lids, ribbon, glue, glitter, and markers.)

Say: **We celebrate Jesus' birth at Christmas time by hanging special decorations in our homes and churches. All the lights and orna-**

ments make people feel happy. **Christmas gives us a special feeling that we could use year-round. So let's make some hope ornaments that we can hang up to make us feel good.**

Give each student a clear plastic lid and some ribbon. Make glue, glitter, and markers available. Say: **As you make your ornament, use colors or symbols or shapes that represent your feelings about the hope Jesus' birth brings. Be ready to share what your ornament stands for.**

Allow about five to 10 minutes for kids to make their ornaments. Then have kids hold up their ornaments for others to see. Ask:

● **How does your ornament remind you of the hope that Jesus' birth brings?**

● **What could you do this week to be like a Christmas ornament—that is, to show someone else that Jesus' birth brought new hope for everyone?**

6. Trimming the Tree

(You'll need a Christmas tree— either a real one or an outline of one made of green construction paper and taped to a wall—the ornaments from the "Hope Ornaments" activity, and tape.)

Gather everyone around a Christmas tree (either a real tree or the outline you have posted on the wall).

Say: **Jesus' birth brought new hope for everyone. That hope can make our lives bright and beautiful, just as ornaments turn an ordinary tree into a bright and beautiful Christmas tree.**

Take a moment to think of a single-sentence prayer—either thanking Jesus for the hope he gives you or committing yourself to sharing that hope this week in a specific way. Then come forward and say your prayer as you hang your ornament on the tree.

Start the prayer yourself, then let kids continue as they hang their ornaments on the real tree or tape them to the construction paper tree on the wall.

Leave the decorated tree up in your classroom for a few weeks as a reminder that Jesus' birth brought new hope for everyone.

13. How a Little Becomes a Lot (Feeding the 5,000)

Lunch for 5,000 from one boy's lunch basket? Providing lunch for 5,000 people is no easy task, even today. But what if you had to do it with just two small fish and five rye cakes? Impossible, you say? Not for Jesus!

Upper-elementary kids want to make a difference in their world, but their youth and limited resources can make them feel insignificant. Use this lesson to help kids learn that their efforts, no matter how small, can be world-changing when teamed with God's power.

A POWERFUL POINT

God can do great things with whatever we have to offer.

A LOOK AT THE LESSON

1. Cookie Contributions (8 minutes)
2. News Flash (15 minutes)
3. No Gift Too Small (8 minutes)
4. Loaves and Fishes (9 minutes)
5. Lunch Bags and Little Fish (5 minutes)
6. Cookie Compliments (5 minutes)

THE FUN-TO-LEARN LESSON

1. Cookie Contributions

(You'll need plain cookies in bags, frosting in containers, plastic knives, and decorative candies in containers.)

As kids arrive, give each person one of the following items: a bag of plain cookies, a container of frosting, a plastic knife, or a container of decorative candies. It's OK for more than one person to get the same item. Be sure that the supplies, when pooled, are sufficient to make two frosted, decorated cookies for each student.

When everyone has arrived, say: **I'd like everyone in our class to get a nice snack. Who can feed our whole class?** Kids will almost certainly realize that they can pool their resources to make a good snack. If they don't figure this out on their own, prompt them.

Let kids decide on their own how they'll get the cookies decorated. For example, distribute what they have; set their supplies out for others to use; or divide the decorating jobs according to who has the appropriate ingredient. Provide a large plate and ask kids to put the finished, decorated cookies on the plate.

When all the cookies are decorated, pass the plate around and let each person take and eat one cookie. Ask:
● **What went through your mind when I asked you to feed the class?**
● **What did you contribute to the cookie you just ate? How did your contribution improve the final product?**

● **Give a real-life example of how something that's small all by itself can contribute to something much bigger or better.**

● **How is that like the way God uses what we have to offer to do his work in the world?**

Say: **God can do great things with whatever we have to offer. Let's examine a familiar story about a boy whose small contribution turned into a newsworthy event.**

2. News Flash

(You'll need paper, pencils, and Bibles.)

Say: **News teams sometimes interrupt our favorite TV programs with important information about a late-breaking, newsworthy event. Today we have our own important story to report on.**

Form groups of no more than three people. Hand out Bibles, paper, and pencils. Have each group select a Scripture reader, a scriptwriter, and a news reporter. Have the readers read John 6:1-15 to their groups.

Say: **Imagine that this story just took place today. Write a special report about the event, similar to the ones we see on television about current events.**

Allow the kids seven minutes to prepare their news flash, then ask the news reporters to "broadcast" their stories. Encourage applause after each presentation.

When all the reporters have presented their newscasts, have the groups discuss the following questions:

● **Who do you think is the "star" of this news story? Explain.**

● **How might the story have been different if the boy had not offered his food for Jesus to use?**

● **How would the story have been**

different if the boy had tried to feed the people without involving Jesus?

● **What can you learn from this event that applies to your life today?**

Say: **God can do great things with whatever we have to offer. The boy with the bread and fish found that out. Let's see what we can learn about ourselves from this event.**

3. No Gift Too Small

Direct students to number off within their groups from one to three. Say: **Discuss the next few questions in your groups. Then I'll call out a number from one to three. The person in your group whose number I call out will be responsible for sharing your answer.**

Ask:

● **What feelings might have kept the boy from offering his bread and fish for Jesus to use?**

● **How did the boy's action show that he had faith in Jesus?** (If students don't mention it themselves, point out that the boy's action not only showed that he trusted Jesus not to rob him of his lunch, but that he had faith that Jesus could turn a little bit of food into a feast.)

● **What are some "little" things—talents, time, material things—you have to offer for Jesus to use?**

● **What could keep you from offering those things?**

● **What would you say to a person who says, "I'm not rich, and I don't have any special talents. I don't have anything God can use"?**

● **When have you seen God do something special with something you gave or a service you offered? How did that make you feel?**

Say: **God can do great things with**

whatever we have to offer. Let's think of some specific things we can offer for God to use.

4. Loaves and Fishes

(You'll need construction paper, scissors, markers, and thumbtacks or transparent tape.)

Form pairs. Hand out construction paper, scissors, and markers.

Say: **Take three minutes to think of physical things you have that you could give to help someone in Jesus' name. For each item you think of, draw or cut a shape of a fish and write that item on the fish.**

After three minutes, have one person from each pair post the fish on the bulletin board or tape them to the wall, reading what is written on each one. For each item, have kids suggest how or where they could give that item. For example, kids could give extra or outgrown clothes to needy kids through a clothing program, or they could put them in a Goodwill box.

Next say: **Now take three minutes to think of abilities you or others in this class have that you could use for Jesus. Think not only of special talents, like being able to play the piano, but of more "ordinary" abilities, like helping your parents or an elderly neighbor with yard work. For each item you think of, draw or cut a shape of a loaf of bread and write that item on the bread.**

After three minutes, have the other person from each pair post the loaves on the bulletin board or tape them to the wall, reading what is written on each one. As each loaf is posted, ask kids to suggest specific opportunities for using the ability listed, like accom-

panying the singing in Sunday school or playing piano for residents of a nursing home.

Ask:

● **How do you feel when you see all the material objects and gifts of time and ability we have to offer?**

● **What do you think might happen if we offered all these things to God to use?**

Say: **God can do great things with whatever we have to offer. Let's let God turn some loaves and fishes into a feast!**

5. Lunch Bags and Little Fish

(You'll need paper lunch bags and the loaves and fishes from the "Loaves and Fishes" activity.)

Hand out paper lunch bags. Have kids gather by the fish and bread shapes they posted on the bulletin board or wall.

Say: **Choose at least one thing from our list that you could give to Jesus this week. Take it off the wall and put it in your lunch bag. If someone has already taken the idea you chose, write the idea on another piece of paper. Take your lunch bag home with you. Keep it somewhere you will see it each day to remind you that God can do great things with whatever we have to offer.**

When everyone has taken at least one loaf or fish, pray: **Lord, today we read about a young boy that gave his lunch to Jesus, and as a result 5,000 people were fed. Today we offer our own gifts to you. We ask that you bless every one. In Jesus' name, amen.**

6. Cookie Compliments

(You'll need the remaining cookies kids decorated during the "Cookie Contributions" activity and Bibles.)

Have kids sit in a circle. Say: **Often we give to Jesus by giving of ourselves to those around us.**

Hand out Bibles and have kids read in unison Matthew 25:40. Ask:

● **How does it make you feel to know that when you help someone else, it's like helping Jesus?**

● **How could this verse affect your attitude toward other people who need your help this week?**

● **How could this verse affect your attitude toward people who do something good for you?**

Get out the remaining cookies the kids decorated at the beginning of the lesson. Pass the plate around and ask each student to pick out a special cookie for the person to his or her right.

Say: **Think of one way you have seen the person to your right do something kind or helpful for another person.** Give kids a few moments to think.

Say: **When it's your turn, hand your cookie to the person on your right and complete this sentence: "I know God can do great things through you because ... "** Fill in the blank with something specific like **"because you go out of your way to be friendly to new people"** or **"because you give your time to help with the little kids in the nursery." I'll start, and we'll go around the circle to the right.**

Give your cookie to the person on your right and affirm that person. Then have that person turn to the next person and so on around the circle.

When everyone has given a cookie and a compliment to the person on the right, say: **God can do great things with whatever we have to offer. God has already started doing great things through you!**

14. Accepting Others
(The Woman at the Well)

We often see kids forming cliques that exclude others who seem different or unacceptable. Children will often tease, taunt, and ridicule those who appear different.

In the story of the woman at the well, we have an opportunity to see how Jesus handled such a problem. Use this lesson to encourage children to accept others.

A POWERFUL POINT

Jesus broke through the barriers of prejudice.

A LOOK AT THE LESSON

1. Clown Mania (12 minutes)
2. Action Reading (10 minutes)
3. Discovery (10 minutes)
4. Paper-Slip Baseball (10 minutes)
5. Action! (8 minutes)
6. You Can Do It (5 minutes)
7. Pass It On! (5 minutes)

THE FUN-TO-LEARN LESSON

1. Clown Mania

(You'll need clown makeup, funny hats, a variety of clothes, and candy for prizes.)

Form groups of no more than four and choose one person in each group to get a goofy makeover. Provide funny hats, clothes, and makeup for each group. Allow five to seven minutes for the makeovers.

Teacher Tip

Clown makeup is available in most costume shops and in many department or drugstores.

Afterward, award candy prizes for the most creative, unique, funny, and interesting makeovers. Give one award to each group and say something positive about each group's makeover. Then ask groups to discuss the following questions. Have the oldest person in each group report answers to the first question, the next oldest report answers to the second question, and so on. Ask:

● **How does it feel to have people in the class who look so different from everyone else?**

● **How would your friends react if you started dressing like this all the time?**

● **How would you feel if your best friend started dressing like this?**

● **How do you think Jesus would react to someone who looks odd or seems different?**

Say: **Often people are left out or rejected because of the color of their skin, the style of clothing they wear, how much money they have, or where they live. That kind of** prejudice isn't new; prejudice was strong way back when Jesus lived on earth. But Jesus broke through the barriers of prejudice. Today we're going to find out how Jesus did it and what it means for us.

Have each group clean up its work area, putting away all hats, makeup, costumes, and so on.

2. Action Reading

(You'll need photocopies of the "Woman at the Well" handout on pages 81 and 82.)

Form four groups: A, B, C, and D. Give each child a copy of the handout "The Woman at the Well."

Say: **Follow along as we read this story. When it's your group's turn, read your lines and do the motions listed in parentheses.**

Point out any words that may be unfamiliar such as "Sychar" (pronounced SIGH-kar) and tell kids how to pronounce them. Then have the groups read the script aloud.

Have kids stand as you ask the following questions. Give kids a few seconds to think after each question and tell them you'd like to hear lots of interesting responses. When one student shares an answer, kids who thought of the same answer and have nothing more to add can sit down. When everyone is seated, ask the next question and repeat the process. (If all the kids sit down after the first student shares an answer, have kids stand up and ask the question again to encourage another response.) Ask:

● **How would you describe the character whose part you played?**

● **Which character did you most relate to? Why?**

● **Why do you think Jesus spoke with the Samaritan woman when other Jewish teachers wouldn't?**

● **Do you ever feel that you have to meet certain standards or requirements in order to be accepted by others? If so, when?**

● **Most of us have read stories that end with a moral. What do you think the moral of this story might be?**

● **How can we apply this moral to our own lives?**

Say: **Jesus broke through the barriers of prejudice. Let's explore this further.**

3. Discovery

(You'll need paper, pencils, and Bibles.)

Form discussion groups of no more than four. Hand out Bibles, paper, and pencils. Have each group assign one person to be the reader who reads the Scripture, one to be the recorder who writes his or her group's responses to the questions, one to be the reporter who'll report answers to the class, and one to be an encourager who urges everyone to participate.

Have the readers read John 4:5-30 aloud to their groups. Then ask:

● **How was the relationship between Jewish people and Samaritan people like cliques in your school?**

● **Share a time when you have felt excluded or ignored, like the Samaritan woman felt.**

● **Share a time when you have gone out of your way to break out of a clique or to include someone, as Jesus did.**

● **Share a time when you were like the disciples, just sort of standing by watching.**

● **If Jesus came to your school, how do you think he would respond to what he saw? Who do you think Jesus would spend time with?**

● **If you were to follow along with Jesus in his visit to your school, and do the things Jesus was doing, how would your day be different?**

Have each group's reporter share the group's responses with the rest of the class.

Say: **Prejudice comes in many forms. Prejudice doesn't just mean judging someone based on race. Prejudice is judging and excluding someone for any reason at all before you even know the person. Jesus broke through the barriers of prejudice. But people still form cliques and groups for all sorts of reasons. Let's look at some of the reasons people use to rate others as winners or losers.**

4. Paper-Slip Baseball

(You'll need two paper grocery sacks, construction paper of several different colors including white, masking tape, newsprint, a marker, and Bibles.)

Before the lesson, fill the two grocery sacks with strips of colored construction paper. You'll need to have at least one white strip of paper for every two colored strips. The other colors don't matter, but it's best to have a variety of at least five or six different colors.

Say: **Today we're going to play a new version of blackboard baseball. Choosing the right color paper strip will determine a hit, a home run, or an out. If you make enough good choices, your team wins. If not, you'll lose!**

Mark out two baseball diamonds on the floor using masking tape. The size of the diamonds doesn't matter, as long as there is room for one person to stand on each base.

Form two teams and have each team line up by home plate at one of the diamonds. Place one of the grocery sacks at each home plate.

The person first in line is "up to bat." Have that person look away from his or her team's sack and then reach in the appropriate bag to select a paper slip, sight unseen. Tell kids that a colored slip of paper gets the batter to first base and a white paper slip is an out. If a batter gets an out, he or she must go to the end of the line.

Teacher Tip

If you wish to add some excitement to the game, use different colors to represent various types of hits. For instance:
● green = single
● black = double
● yellow = triple
● red = home run!

Give each team seven minutes to play. Then tally the number of runs batted in to determine the winning team.

After the game, have each person find a partner from the opposing team to form pairs for discussion. Have pairs review the story in John 4:5-30, then discuss their answers to the questions that follow. (Write the questions on newsprint for kids to refer to during discussions.)

● **What was your reaction when someone on your team drew a white paper slip?**

● **How did you respond when your teammates drew a paper slip that had a color on it?**

● **If you were to choose one paper slip to represent the woman in our story, which color slip would you choose? Why?**

● **How can the color of your skin or your cultural background affect** the way others treat and accept you?

● **What do you think affects the way Jesus treats and accepts you? How can you follow his example this week?**

After a few minutes of discussion, have the person wearing the most green in each pair report one or two insights about the lesson gained from answering the questions.

Ask each student to pick out one last paper slip. Say: **For the next 60 seconds we're going to pray silently for God to show us how to share the love of Jesus with the people around us. If you have a red paper slip, pray about your family; a white paper slip, pray for your friends; a black paper slip, pray for your teachers.**

Teacher Tip

If you don't have paper slips that are red or black, substitute any other color you used in the game for the prayer.

After one minute, pray: **Jesus, thank you that you broke through the barriers of prejudice. Help us to show that same kind of love to the people around us. In your name we pray, amen.**

5. Action!

Say: **Jesus broke through the barriers of prejudice when he sat down and talked with the woman at the well. That wasn't a complicated or difficult solution. Let's come up with some practical ways to break down prejudice in our everyday lives.**

Form groups of five. Say: **In your group, think of a situation you might see this week in which**

someone is being excluded or rejected.

For example, you might think of a new person at school who doesn't have any friends to sit with at lunch. Come up with at least one realistic way that you could include that person. Your plan doesn't have to be anything flashy; it could be as simple as inviting the person to sit with you. After all, that's what Jesus did! Then prepare to act out the situation and your solution for the rest of the class.

Give kids four or five minutes to prepare and practice their dramatizations, then call on each group to perform. After every group is done, ask:

● **Which of these situations have you observed in real life?**

● **How did you respond?**

● **Which of these solutions have you used? How well did it work?**

● **What keeps people from acting on these simple solutions?**

● **If you're the person who feels left out, how can you use these solutions?** If kids don't suggest it, point out that we often focus only on the group we want to get "in" with. Challenge kids to look for others who are also feeling left out and focus on including them.

● **Which of these situations (or a similar situation) might you face this week?**

● **What will it take for you to try one of these solutions?** If kids are stumped, suggest such possibilities as teaming up with someone from this class for moral support or praying for courage.

Say: **Jesus broke through the barriers of prejudice. You can, too!**

6. You Can Do It

(You'll need paper, pencils, and colored markers.)

Form a circle. Pass out paper, pencils, and colored markers.

Say: **You have special qualities and abilities that equip you to break through the barriers of prejudice and reach out to others. So do the people around you.**

Ask students to create a card for the person to their left. Have students fold paper to form a card. Then say: **Write, "You can do it" on the front of the card. On the inside write, "because..."** Fill in the blank with a positive quality about that person. For example, "You can do it because your friendly smile makes people feel welcome," "You can do it because others follow your lead," or "You can do it because you care enough about people to reach out."

Once the cards are finished, say: **One at a time we're going to share our cards of appreciation. Tell us who you made your card for and what you think is special about that person.**

Allow students to give the cards to the appropriate people, then say: **Jesus broke through the barriers of prejudice. You can, too!**

7. Pass It On!

(You'll need a paper bag and individually wrapped candy.)

Place some individually wrapped candy in a paper bag.

Remain in a circle and say: **Today I've brought some candy for you. As the bag of candy is passed to you, share one thing you have learned during our time together, then help yourself to a piece of candy. Then pass the bag to the person on your left.**

Kids may say things like "I learned that I need to try to include others more" or "I discovered that it is important to show people I care about them."

Conclude by saying: **Jesus broke through the barriers of prejudice. You can, too!**

THE WOMAN AT THE WELL

Based on John 4:5-30

Directions: Each group must read and do the actions written for its assigned character.

Group A—Narrator

Group C—Jesus

Group B—Disciples

Group D—Woman

THE SCRIPT

NARRATOR: *(Stand and walk in place as though very tired.)* Jesus was on a long journey with his disciples from Judea to Galilee, but on the way he had to pass through a country named Samaria.

DISCIPLES: We were near the town of Sychar, where the field Jacob had given to Joseph is located. *(Point toward the other side of the room.)* Jacob's well was there. *(Pretend to draw water from the well.)*

JESUS: *(Stand, pause to rub your eyes, yawn, and stretch. Then sit down.)* I became tired and sat down to rest beside the well. It must have been nearly 12 o'clock.

NARRATOR: *(Stand and shake your head and index finger at Jesus.)* Jewish law forbids teachers to speak to women, Samaritans, or sinners. That's why it's so hard to believe what happened next.

WOMAN: *(Stand and pretend you are drawing water from the well.)* I was on my way to Jacob's well to get some water. You can imagine my surprise when I found a Jewish teacher resting near the well. The Jews rarely traveled through Samaria. What was even more surprising was that he asked me for a drink!

DISCIPLES: *(Stand and rub your stomach as though hungry.)* We would have gotten the water for him ourselves, but we were not there. We were all so hungry, we went into town to buy some food.

WOMAN: *(Stand up and point toward Jesus while shaking your head.)* I just couldn't believe this man would ask me for a drink.

JESUS: *(Stand up and pace back and forth before speaking, as though deep in thought.)* I told her, "If only you knew who I was, you would ask me for the living water."

WOMAN: I'd never heard of living water before. I asked him where this water might be and how he would obtain it for me. Listen to what he said. *(Hold hand up to ear as though listening.)*

THE WOMAN AT THE WELL

Everyone who drinks of my water will never be thirsty again. *(Everyone in class pretends to be drinking the water.)* The water that I have to give will spring up inside of you giving you eternal life. *(Everyone in class jumps up and down, clapping.)*

WOMAN: I knew right then and there that I wanted some of this living water. *(Pretend to shake Jesus to get his attention and then hold out your hand for the water.)*

NARRATOR: *(Hold your hand up to your mouth and whisper loudly.)* The woman became very sad, however, when Jesus made his next request.

JESUS: Go and get your husband and bring him back here with you.

WOMAN: *(Throw hands in the air as you jump up.)* I don't have a husband. What shall I do?

JESUS: You have answered correctly. You have no husband. You've had five husbands, but the man you live with now is not your husband. *(Hold up five fingers and shake your head.)*

NARRATOR: She knew right away that this man must be a prophet. How else could he know so much about her? *(Point to the woman.)*

DISCIPLES: *(Walk in place pre-tending to be carrying food.)* We were on our way back to the well with the food we had bought when we saw Jesus! We couldn't believe our eyes! He was talking to a Samaritan woman about worship! *(Jump up and down, pointing at the woman.)*

JESUS: *(Stand and wave hand over the disciples to quiet them.)* You Samaritans worship something you don't even know. We understand what we worship, for salvation comes from the Jews.

NARRATOR: He went on to tell her that the time was coming when true worshipers would worship the Father in spirit and truth, and that time is already here. *(Stand and fold hands as if in prayer.)*

WOMAN: I know that when the Messiah comes he will explain all this to us. *(Pretend to pick up jar as if to go.)*

JESUS: *(Stands up and points to himself.)* I am he—I, the one talking to you now.

NARRATOR: The woman picked up her jar and went back to town. She told everyone she saw about Jesus. Soon the people left the town and came to the well. They wanted to see this man named Jesus.

Permission to photocopy this handout from *Fun-to-Learn Bible Lessons: Grades 4 & Up* granted for local church use. Copyright © Group Publishing, Inc., Box 481, Loveland, CO 80539.

15. Jesus Did It—He Won!
(Jesus)

The Bible unfolds as a great drama that climaxes in the death and resurrection of Jesus Christ. That climax is the turning point of all history. And although we continue to face tense battles, the deciding battle of the cosmic conflict was won on that first Easter Sunday.

Kids want to be on the winning team. What better team than God's? Kids need to know the power of Jesus' resurrection—that sin and death were defeated. That knowledge puts a whole new twist on reality. When things are going well, they can praise God for the good times. And when times get tough, they need to know that Jesus' followers are assured the ultimate victory. We know who wins! And we're on God's team!

A POWERFUL POINT

Jesus defeated sin and death when he died and rose again.

A LOOK AT THE LESSON

1. Hail to the Victors! (7 minutes)
2. Special Effects (15 minutes)
3. Real Life (10 minutes)
4. Bounce Back (13 minutes)
5. Roll the Stone (10 minutes)
6. Exit Winners (3 minutes)

THE FUN-TO-LEARN LESSON

1. Hail to the Victors!

(You'll need newsprint, masking tape, and markers.)

Before class, tape together sheets of newsprint to make a 4-foot banner. Seat kids in a circle on the floor, and ask:

● **Have you ever been to a football game where the home team is introduced as they rush onto the field? How did the crowd react?**

● **How do you suppose the players feel when they enter the playing field and hear the cheers of the crowd?**

Say: **When the crowd welcomes the team that way, it's as if they're saying, "We believe in you! We think you're winners!" Well, I believe in all of you, and I think you're winners. Not as a football team—although some of you may be pretty good at that, too—but as God's people. Let's start this class by giving each other a victor's welcome.**

Spread out a 4-foot-long sheet of newsprint on the floor. In the center write, "Welcome, winners!" Give each person a marker.

Say: **Write your name somewhere on this sheet. Then find someone else's name and write by his or her name one reason you think that** person is a winner. You could note something the person is good at, like soccer or playing the piano, or you could name a positive quality the person has, like friendliness or a good sense of humor. Or you could jot down something special the person has done, like helping you with a project. You may write by as many names as you like, but every name needs to have at least three things written by it.

Give kids about four minutes to write, then have them find their own names and read silently the comments other kids wrote. Ask:

● **Which comment surprised you the most?**

● **Which comment makes you feel most like a winner?**

Say: **Today we're going to explore the greatest story about winning ever told—the story of how Jesus defeated sin and death when he died and rose again.**

Put the banner away for later use in this lesson.

2. Special Effects

(You'll need Bibles.)

Form five groups. A group can be as small as two people or as large as 20. (If you have fewer than 10 students, form groups of two and assign each group more than one passage.)

Assign each group one of the following passages:

● Group 1—Mark 15:6-11
● Group 2—Mark 15:19-21
● Group 3—Mark 15:22-25
● Group 4—Mark 15:33-39
● Group 5—Mark 16:1-8

Say: **Imagine that you have been hired to provide a soundtrack for this passage. Choose one person to read your passage aloud to your group. Then make up some back-**ground music or sounds to go along with the words. Think about setting the mood for your part of the story. Once each group has its soundtrack planned, I will read the story, and you can all put your sounds together to orchestrate it.**

Give each group five minutes to work out music and sounds to go with their passage. Then call everyone together. Have groups sit in the order that their passages appear. Read aloud each passage and signal each group to perform its soundtrack as you read the assigned verses.

Afterward, assign each student one of the following questions:

● **What emotions were you trying to communicate with your soundtrack?**

● **What incidents struck you as especially dramatic in this story?**

● **Who would you say are the "bad guys" in this story? Who are the "good guys"?**

● **How did Jesus' death affect his friends?**

● **How did Jesus' coming to life again affect his friends?**

● **How does Jesus' death and coming to life again affect you?**

Say: **You've got three minutes to quickly interview two or more people in this room to discover their answers to the question you've been assigned. Go!**

When three minutes are up, allow several kids to report the results of their interviews. Be sure each interview question gets reported on at least once. Then say: **Jesus didn't just win a victory over Pilate, the soldiers, and the other bad guys in the story. Jesus defeated sin and death when he died and rose again. Let's explore what that victory means for us today.**

3. Real Life

(You'll need paper, pencils, and Bibles.)

Have students form pairs. Distribute paper and pencils. Assign half the pairs Isaiah 53:11 and Luke 24:44-49. Assign the other half 1 Corinthians 15:17 and 20-22.

Say: **Read your verses and write your answers to my questions. Make sure you both write your answers because in a few minutes you'll share your responses with someone from one of the other pairs.**

Teacher Tip

To make discussions flow more easily, write the questions on newsprint for kids to refer to during discussion times.

Ask:

● **Why do you think it was necessary for Christ to rise from the dead?**

● **How was it possible for Jesus to do that?**

● **What would happen if Jesus hadn't risen from the dead?**

● **How does (or could) the fact that Jesus rose from the dead affect your daily life?**

When the pairs have discussed these questions, say: **Now find a new partner who read the other passage.**

When the new pairs have formed, have them read their passages to each other. Then repeat the questions, having the new partners share their responses.

Say: **When Jesus gave his life on the cross, he carried all of our sins with him. Jesus died so we could be forgiven by God. When Jesus rose from the dead, he conquered death. Jesus won the battle, so we** can celebrate the victory! And we can tell others how exciting it is to be on the winning team! Jesus defeated sin and death when he died and rose again.**

4. Bounce Back

(You'll need a Ping-Pong ball and a cup of water.)

Seat kids in a semicircle. Say: **The exciting story of Jesus' victory over sin and death deserves to be told in an exciting way. This is your chance to come up with a creative and interesting way to tell about Jesus' death and resurrection. You can use anything you find in this classroom. But first let me give you an example of what I mean.**

Take out the Ping-Pong ball and the cup half full of water.

Say: **With the items you see here, I'm going to tell you the story of Jesus' death and resurrection. This Ping-Pong ball represents Jesus; the cup is the world we live in; and the water is death. As Jesus was put to death** (push the Ping-Pong ball down into the water and hold it there), **he gave his life for us. But death couldn't hold him for long. After three days he rose** (release the ball and let it bounce out of the cup) **from the dead. He defeated sin and death forever!**

Form groups of four. Allow kids up to five minutes to meet together in their small groups to decide how they will present their object lesson. Remind kids they can use anything in the room, including anything they brought into the room. Then give each group an opportunity to tell its story.

After the last group has presented its story, have students number off within their groups from one to four. Say: **Discuss the next few questions** in your groups. Then I'll call out a number from one to four. The person in your group whose number I call out will be responsible for sharing your group's answer.

Ask:

● What items would have been easier to use to tell this story?

● How would you explain Jesus' death and resurrection to a friend?

● What parts of the story do you have questions about? How would others in class answer those questions?

5. Roll the Stone

(You'll need small stones, markers, and Bibles.)

Say: **Let's explore more about this story of Jesus' resurrection.**

Form a circle. Ask each person to respond to each question with a one-word answer:

● What would it have been like to be present at Jesus' crucifixion?

● What would it have been like to be present at Jesus' empty tomb?

● What one word describes how your life would have changed if you had witnessed Jesus' death and resurrection?

● What one word describes how your life has been affected by simply hearing the news of Jesus' death and resurrection?

Say: **Jesus' death and resurrection mark the turning point for all history. Jesus defeated sin and death when he died and rose again. He won!**

Read aloud Mark 16:1-3. Say: **When the women went to Jesus' tomb on Easter morning, they were worried about who would roll away the stone from in front of the cave. That stone was a big problem for them.**

Give a small stone to everyone and make markers available for kids to use. Say: **All of us have a stone or two in our lives that we'd like to roll away, but we're not strong enough to do it alone. Think about one problem or situation in your life where you could use God's help.** Share an area in your own life in which you need God's guidance. Be as open as possible to set an example of honesty.

Say: **Choose a situation that you are willing to share with the rest of the group, then write one word or draw a symbol on your stone to describe the situation.**

When everyone has drawn or written on a stone, read aloud Mark 16:4. Say: **When the women got to Jesus' tomb, the heavy stone had been moved for them. They didn't have the strength to move it, but the risen Jesus did. He has the power to roll away our "stones," too.**

Have everyone stand in the circle. Have each person briefly share what he or she wrote or drew. Then say: **Now everyone pass your stone to the person on your right. Look at the word or symbol on the new stone. If you don't remember what the person's concern is, ask the person who gave the stone to you. We're going to pray for each other now. I'll start by praying for the request on** (name of person to your right)**'s stone, and then that person will continue the prayer for the next person to the right.**

After the prayer, say: **Take your stone home as a reminder that God will move the stones in your life. He can do it because Jesus defeated sin and death when he died and rose again!**

6. Exit Winners

(You'll need the banner from the "Hail to the Victors!" activity and masking tape.)

Say: **As we leave this room today, we'll be entering a world full of problems and trials. But because Jesus defeated sin and death when he died and rose again, we can walk out of here as winners. So, let's make a winner's entrance into the rest of our week the same way a ball team makes a winner's entrance on-to the field.**

Have everyone stand quietly just inside the door while you tape the newsprint banner across the doorway. To avoid ripping any kids' names when you run through the banner, tape it so the word "welcome" is in the middle of the doorway. On your signal, have everyone run out the door, breaking through the paper.

Afterward, let kids tear out and keep their names and the positive things others wrote about them. Throw out the rest of the banner.

16. God's Present, God's Presence (The Holy Spirit)

God can seem far away to kids. When there's no one to talk to, their locker combination doesn't work, and church seems boring, God's Spirit is just the gift kids need. The Holy Spirit can help kids remember important things about Jesus. He can comfort them when they're sad. He can lead and direct their lives. Kids need the Holy Spirit to be real in their lives. This lesson can introduce the Spirit as a gift from God. And who is going to turn down a gift like that?

A POWERFUL POINT

The Holy Spirit is a present we can enjoy every day.

A LOOK AT THE LESSON

1. Gift Grab (5 minutes)
2. Special Delivery (10 minutes)
3. Spirit Powered (8 minutes)
4. Remember Relay (7 minutes)
5. Spiritual Fruit Basket Upset (7 minutes)
6. You've Got A-Peal (10 minutes)
7. Pass the Light (4 minutes)

THE FUN-TO-LEARN LESSON

1. Gift Grab

(You'll need gift-wrapped boxes that are empty.)

As students arrive, hand each person a gift-wrapped package. Tell kids not to open the packages yet.

When everyone has arrived, say: **If you'd like to trade your package for someone else's, you now have two minutes to try to get the package you'd really rather have. However, trades must be made by mutual consent, which means no grabbing or taking someone else's package without that person's OK to trade with you!**

Let kids trade for two minutes. Then have everyone sit in a circle and examine their gift boxes, but don't let kids open them yet. Ask:

● **Why did you choose the package you did? What made it appealing?**

● **What do you hope is in the package?**

● **If you could choose an invisible present—like happiness, love, or security—what would you choose?**

● **How would that invisible present make your life better?**

Allow kids to open their boxes. Then ask:

● **How is the Holy Spirit like an invisible present?**

● **How can the Holy Spirit make your life better?**

Teacher Tip

Some kids may have never heard of the Holy Spirit. After kids open their boxes, you may want to start off with the question, "What can you tell me about the Holy Spirit?" Then, based on your church or denomination's doctrinal statement, give a brief explanation of who the Holy Spirit is before moving into the body of the lesson.

Say: **The Holy Spirit is a present we can enjoy every day. Let's find out how God first delivered that present.**

2. Special Delivery

(You'll need Bibles.)

Form groups of four. Direct students to number off within their groups from one to four. Have all the ones read aloud Acts 2:1-8, all the twos read Acts 2:12-18, all the threes read Acts 2:22-24, and all the fours read Acts 2:32-47.

Say: **Discuss the next few questions in your groups. Then I'll call out a number from one to four. The person in your group whose number I call out will be responsible for sharing your answer.**

Ask:

● **If you had heard the sound of wind and seen the flames, what would you have thought and felt?**

● **What do you suppose went through Jesus' followers' minds when they began talking in languages they had never learned?**

● **Why do you think it was easier for some people to believe the apostles were drunk than to believe that the apostles were filled with the Holy Spirit?**

● **What makes it hard for people to believe in the power of the Holy Spirit today?**

● **If you had been present in this story, what would you have thought about the Holy Spirit?**

● **How do you feel about the promise given in verses 38 and 39?**

● **According to verse 38, what do you have to do to receive the Holy Spirit as a gift? What do you think that means in everyday actions?**

Say: **When God gave the Holy Spirit at that first Pentecost, people heard and saw some of the Spirit's power in the wind and the flames and the languages. Many were eager to receive the Holy Spirit and the Spirit's power. The Holy Spirit is a present we can enjoy every day, too. Let's explore how the Holy Spirit's power affects our lives today.**

3. Spirit Powered

(You'll need photocopies of the "Spirit Powered" handout on page 93, pencils, and Bibles.)

Give each foursome a copy of the "Spirit Powered" handout and a pencil. Have each foursome appoint one reader to look up and read the Bible passages, another reader to read the case studies and the questions aloud in the small group, a recorder to write the group's answers to the questions, and a reporter to share those answers with the rest of the class.

The correct matches are:

1. John 14:26 and 1 Corinthians 2:12—Teacher

2. Acts 9:31 and Philippians 2:1-2—Encourager/Comforter

3. John 16:13 and Acts 16:7—Leader/Guide

Allow the groups about five minutes to read and complete the handout. Then have the reporters each share their group's ideas with the class.

Say: **The Holy Spirit is a present**

we can enjoy every day. Jesus promised that the Holy Spirit would help us by teaching us and reminding us of how Jesus wants us to live. Let's look at that promise.

4. Remember Relay

(You'll need paper, pencils, and a Bible.)

Form two teams and have each team line up in single file. (If you have fewer than six students, form one line and have the kids race against the clock as they complete this relay.) Hand the first person in each line a folded piece of paper on which you have written John 14:26. Warn kids not to unfold the paper until you give the signal.

Say: **When I say "go," open the paper, read the verse, and study it for as long as it takes to memorize it. Then pass the paper to the teammate next to you, run to me, and recite the verse from memory. If someone from the opposite team is reciting to me, you must wait until that person is finished. The team that finishes first is the winning team.**

> **Teacher Tip**
> Memorizing the verse in such short time and under pressure will be difficult for most of the kids—that's part of the fun of the game. However, watch carefully to make sure that no one feels put down if they're not able to memorize the verse right away. Set the tone for the class by your encouraging attitude and responses to kids.

Stand between the two teams, give the signal for the relay to start, and let kids complete the relay. Afterward,

have the two teams (still facing each other) move to the center of the room.

Say: **The person facing you on the other team is now your partner.**

Have pairs join together and sit on the floor. Give each pair one of the following questions to discuss (it's OK if more than one pair has the same question). Ask:

● **What made it hard to complete the relay? What would have made it easier?**

● **How would you summarize John 14:26?**

● **How was remembering John 14:26 like remembering the things you've learned about Jesus?**

● **Share a situation in which you could use the Holy Spirit's help in knowing what Jesus would want you to do.**

● **How would it affect your life if you asked the Holy Spirit to help you in your actions and decisions this week?**

> **Teacher Tip**
> If you have fewer than five pairs, assign each pair more than one question.

Allow about two minutes for discussion time. Then have pairs take turns telling the class about their assigned question(s) and answers.

Afterward, say: **The Holy Spirit is a present we can enjoy every day. As the Holy Spirit teaches us and reminds us of how Jesus wants us to live, others begin to see the difference in our lives. Let's look at how the Holy Spirit can change people.**

5. Spiritual Fruit Basket Upset

(You'll need chairs and Bibles.)

Have kids sit in chairs in a circle. Make sure the circle has no empty chairs. You should stand. Hand out Bibles and ask everyone to turn to Galatians 5:22-23.

Say: **In a moment, we're going to play Fruit Basket Upset. Usually in Fruit Basket Upset, players get the names of different kinds of fruit. But today we're going to use the names of what the Bible calls "the fruit of the Spirit." Look at the qualities listed in Galatians 5:22-23. We'll go around the circle and assign each person a quality that is one of the fruits of the Spirit. Make sure you remember what your assigned quality is because you'll keep that quality for the whole game, no matter where you end up sitting.**

Point to a person in the circle and start with "love." Then move around the circle, pointing to each person in turn and having that person read the next quality that makes up the fruit of the Spirit listed in Galatians 5:22-23. Remind kids that the quality they read will be their assigned quality for the entire game.

Teacher Tip

According to Galatians 5:22-23, the Spirit produces the fruit of love, joy, peace, patience, kindness, goodness, faithfulness, gentleness, and self-control.

If you have fewer than nine kids, go around the circle again until every quality listed in Galatians 5:22-23 has been assigned. (Some kids will have more than one quality.) When everyone is ready, have kids put the Bibles under their chairs.

Stand in the middle of the circle and say: **When I call your assigned quality, stand up and find a new chair to sit in. While you're changing chairs, I'm going to try to find a chair. Whoever is left without a chair stands in the middle and calls out of one or more of the assigned qualities that make up the fruit of the Spirit.**

For this game to work, at least two people must stand up each time. If you have fewer than 18 players, be sure the person in the middle calls out at least two qualities each time.

Play the game for three or four minutes. Then tell everyone to be seated in the chairs.

Say: **Discuss my questions with the person next to you. Then I'll call the name of a quality listed in Galatians 5:22-23, and all the people who had that quality for the game will share their responses.**

Ask:

● **What was the secret to success in this game?**

● **How might having the "fruit" listed in Galatians 5:22-23 help you succeed in real life?**

● **When you were in the middle, how could it have helped you to know which person had a particular quality?**

● **How do your everyday actions tell others whether or not you have a quality listed in Galatians 5:22-23?**

● **How could expressing the fruit of the Spirit in your life help someone else this week?**

Say: **When we have the Holy Spirit in our lives, not only can we enjoy the difference, but so can other people! Let's spend some time identifying the fruit of the Spirit in each other.**

6. You've Got A-Peal

(You'll need some fruit such as bananas or grapefruit, markers, and Bibles.)

Form groups of no more than three. Hand out Bibles and markers and give each person a banana or a grapefruit.

Say: **Write your name on your piece of fruit. Write small enough so there is enough room for the other two people in your group to write on your fruit, too.**

Next, have the person whose birthday is closest to today pass his or her fruit to the right in your group. Have everyone else take turns writing one of the nine qualities listed in Galatians 5:22-23 on the fruit that describes the person whose name is on the fruit.

Afterward, take turns telling why you wrote what you did. For example, you might say, "John, I wrote faithfulness because you always come to every activity here at church." Then repeat the process for every person in your group.

When all the groups are done, say:

The Holy Spirit is a present we can enjoy every day. When we let the fruit of the Spirit show in our lives, others can enjoy the Spirit, too.

7. Pass the Light

(You'll need a penlight flashlight.)

Form a circle. Take a penlight flashlight and turn it on. Ask everyone to bow their heads and be in an attitude of prayer. Say: **We're going to pass this light around as a reminder of the Holy Spirit shining in our lives. As you hold the light, say a prayer thanking God for the gift of the Holy Spirit.**

Begin the prayer, then pass the penlight to the person next to you. After everyone has held the light and prayed, close with: **Lord, your Holy Spirit is a present we can enjoy every day. Thank you for the way the Holy Spirit helps us. Thank you for the fruit of the Spirit in our lives. Help us to be bright lights to our friends so they will want to receive this great gift, too. Amen.**

Spirit
POWERED

Directions: *Read the Bible passages below and match them with the jobs of the Holy Spirit in the right column. Then read each of the four situations that follow and discuss the accompanying questions.*

BIBLE PASSAGES

1. John 14:26 and 1 Corinthians 2:12
2. Acts 9:31 and Philippians 2:1-2
3. John 16:13 and Acts 16:7

JOBS OF THE HOLY SPIRIT

___ Encourager/Comforter

___ Leader/Guide

___ Teacher

SITUATION #1—Your friend isn't a Christian, but she's interested in learning more about why you go to church. She's been asking you a lot of questions about the Bible, church, and Jesus. You don't think you can help.
- What job(s) that the Holy Spirit does could help in this situation?
- What would the Holy Spirit do?
- How could you help the Holy Spirit work?

SITUATION #2—You have a big test tomorrow. You studied really hard, but you're nervous. You stayed up late, and now you're worried that you won't do well. You're going crazy!
- What job(s) that the Holy Spirit does could help in this situation?
- What would the Holy Spirit do?
- How could you help the Holy Spirit work?

SITUATION #3—Your best friend's father just got a great job. He'll make lots more money. Your friend's family is so excited, but it means your friend will have to move out of town right away. You've been friends for six years. You'll be totally lost without your best friend. You both want to cry. It's awful.
- What job(s) that the Holy Spirit does could help in this situation?
- What would the Holy Spirit do?
- How could you help the Holy Spirit work?

SITUATION #4—Sometimes when you try to pray at night, you feel like no one is listening. Why would God want to hear your prayers? You feel depressed and sad about school, and your parents are on you all the time. You feel really down.
- What job(s) that the Holy Spirit does could help in this situation?
- What would the Holy Spirit do?
- How could you help the Holy Spirit work?

Permission to photocopy this handout from *Fun-to-Learn Bible Lessons: Grades 4 & Up* granted for local church use. Copyright © Group Publishing, Inc., Box 481, Loveland, CO 80539.

17. From Saul to Paul (Paul)

Many of us know of the Apostle Paul and the books he wrote in the New Testament. Paul's love for Jesus shone powerfully through both his writings and the way he lived. This wasn't always the case, however. Once recognized as a zealous Hebrew scholar, Paul was an enemy of the early Christians. Fortunately, his meeting with Jesus on the road to Damascus changed all that.

Just as Paul was transformed from sinner to saint, we, too, can be changed. In this lesson, students will learn how Jesus can change their lives.

A POWERFUL POINT

Knowing Jesus can change your life.

A LOOK AT THE LESSON

1. Aim for Success (10 minutes)
2. Distorted Truth (10 minutes)
3. Exploration (10 minutes)
4. Eraser Miracle (8 minutes)
5. Getting to Know You (5 minutes)
6. Fresh Starts (10 minutes)

THE FUN-TO-LEARN LESSON

1. Aim for Success

(You'll need a chalkboard and chalk, masking tape, four beanbags, jellybeans, and a blindfold.)

Draw a clown's face with a big nose on the chalkboard. Under the picture write "Success." Make an X with masking tape on the floor approximately six feet in front of the clown's face.

Form two teams. Say: **This clown's name is Success. We're going to play a game with him. The object of this game is to hit Success right on the nose! To make this a little more exciting, you'll wear a blindfold while you throw four beanbags at the clown's face.**

Once you are blindfolded, stand on the X and throw at the clown's face. Each time you are successful in hitting Success on the nose, I will put a jellybean in your team's jar. The team with the most jellybeans at the end is the winner.

Teacher Tip

It's easy to make your own beanbags! Simply pour uncooked beans into a clean sock, then tie a knot in the end of the sock. Create as many beanbags as you need.

Blindfold the first player and let the person throw each of the four beanbags. For every direct hit, put a jellybean in that team's jar. Continue to play, alternating members from the two teams.

After everyone has tried this game with the blindfold, play it again without the blindfold. Reward kids with a jellybean treat. Then ask:

● **How did it feel to wear a blindfold while trying to play this game? Explain.**

● **Wearing a blindfold is like walking around in the dark. How would you feel if the lights went out right now and it was completely dark in this room?**

● **What would it be like to look for candles or flashlights without the aid of a light?**

● **How could a friend with a flashlight make a difference?**

Say: **Knowing Jesus is like having a friend with a flashlight in a dark place. When we feel lost or alone and can't see which way to turn, Jesus shines the light of his love on our lives. Knowing Jesus can change your life. Let's find out how.**

2. Distorted Truth

(You'll need paper, a marker, tape, a pair of inexpensive binoculars, and Bibles.)

Have kids sit at one end of the room. Use a marker to write the word "truth" on a sheet of paper. The word should be small enough so kids can't read it from across the room. Tape the paper on the wall on the far side of the room and cover it with another sheet of paper.

Say: **I have written a special word on this piece of paper.** Uncover the paper, then say: **Without coming any closer, how many of you can read it?** Pause.

Since no one can read the word, I have a pair of binoculars with me. Look through the binoculars at the word, but don't tell anyone what you see.

Teacher Tip

You can find inexpensive, usable plastic binoculars at most toy stores. You could also substitute a toy telescope for this activity. If neither binoculars nor a telescope are available, have kids look through a sheet of rolled-up paper to see if they can make out the word on the wall.

Pass the binoculars from one student to another until everyone has had a chance to look. Some students may need assistance in focusing the binoculars. Once everyone has seen the word, ask:

● **Why couldn't our eyes see the word at first?**

● **How did the binoculars help us see the word more clearly?**

● **How is looking at the word "truth" without binoculars like trying to understand God's "truth" without help from Jesus?**

Say: **Even though the word "truth" was right in front of us, we needed help to see it. The Apostle Paul had a similar problem. He tried to follow God's truth but got it all wrong. Paul needed someone to help him see. Jesus helped Paul see the truth, and Paul's whole life was changed. Knowing Jesus can change your life, too.**

Let's find out how Paul met Jesus and was changed forever by reading his story in Acts 9:1-19.

3. Exploration

(You'll need paper, markers, and Bibles.)

Form groups of no more than three. Distribute Bibles, paper, and markers. Ask one person in each group to read aloud Acts 9:1-19 to the rest of the group.

Then say: **Use the information in this story to make a comic strip with stick-figure characters. Be sure to include scenes that depict Paul's life before he met Jesus, when he met Jesus on the road, and how Jesus changed his life at the end of the story.**

Allow five minutes for groups to work, then have groups explain their comic strips to the class. Then ask:

● **What do you like most about this story?**

● **How would you have felt if you were Saul and Jesus came to meet you?**

● **Would you like for Jesus to meet you? Why or why not?**

● **What kind of a person was Saul in the beginning of our story?**

● **In what way was Paul changed after he met Jesus?**

● **Why do you think people change once they know Jesus?**

Have kids quickly turn to a partner and say, "Jesus loves you and wants to know you." Then say: **Saul was so changed by his experience on the road to Damascus that he changed his name from Saul to Paul. Knowing Jesus can change your life, too. Let's find out how.**

4. Eraser Miracle

(You'll need wax paper, a permanent marker, tape, colored chalk, a damp cloth, and Bibles.)

Tape a large sheet of wax paper to the wall (or on the chalkboard). Use a permanent marker to draw the outline of a person on the wax paper. (If you aren't artistically inclined, lay the wax paper on the floor and ask one of the students to lie on it while you outline him or her with the marker. However, be careful not to mark that person's clothes or the floor.)

Say: **In his lifetime, Paul did many things wrong. We all do things that are wrong, don't we? Think of things kids sometimes do that are wrong. This might include disobeying parents or teachers, being mean to brothers or sisters, and so on.**

Ask each person to lightly write one of these "wrongs" on the body outline with a piece of colored chalk. Once the list is finished, say: **Before we started listing these "wrongs," this wax-paper person was clean. But now look at it—it's full of sin!**

Ask:

● **How is this person on the wax paper like us in real life?**

● **Once we have these sins in our lives, can they ever be taken away? Why or why not?**

Open your Bible to 1 John 1:8-9. Say: **As I read this passage, listen to what it says about our "wrongs," or sins.** Read the passage, then ask:

● **What does this passage say about the sins we commit?**

● **How does being forgiven for our sins make us different inside?**

Use the damp cloth to wipe away the list of sins on the wax-paper outline. Then say: **Once Paul met Jesus, he was never the same again. Jesus changed him by wiping clean all the wrongs Paul had ever done. When we ask for God's forgiveness, Jesus comes and changes us, too, by forgiving our sins and giving us a new life to share with him. Knowing Jesus can change your life.**

Now let's find out how you can get to know Jesus for yourself.

5. Getting to Know You

Say: **Choose a partner that you don't know very well. You'll have three minutes to learn as much as** you can about your partners. For example, where they live, what they like to eat, what they like to do for fun, and so on.

After three minutes, ask students to share what they learned about their partners with the rest of the class. Then ask:

● **What's it like to get to know somebody new?**

● **How did you learn more about your partner just now?**

● **How might that be like the way you get to know Jesus?**

● **What are some ways you can get to know Jesus this week?**

Say: **Today we got to know one another better by spending time together and asking questions. We can use this same method to get to know Jesus. Jesus wants to know you. He wants to forgive you for all your "wrongs" and give you a new life. Knowing Jesus will most definitely change your life!**

6. Fresh Starts

(You'll need the wax-paper outline of the person you used in the "Eraser Miracle" activity, colored markers, and Bibles.)

Write the Scripture found in 2 Corinthians 5:17 on the wax paper next to the person's outline. Give each student a colored marker. Say: **Look around the room at all the people and pick out at least three "cool Christlike qualities" that different people in this room possess. For example,** you might say a particular person has a great sense of humor. That's a cool Christlike quality.

As I point to you, I want you to call out a cool quality that you see in someone else in the room, then write that quality in our wax-paper person's outline. Then tell us who the quality belongs to.

Allow kids a few minutes to think of three qualities, then start pointing out kids to come forward and write their "cool Christlike qualities" in the outline. Frequently call out qualities you see in kids as well, especially if one or two kids seem to be overlooked by the rest of the class. Continue until everyone gets named at least once.

Ask kids to put their arms around one another and huddle up next to the wax-paper list of cool qualities. Then say: **Jesus has already touched our lives in many ways. Just look at this list! Perhaps Jesus has met you through your parents, your relatives, your friends, or just in your own heart. Jesus loves to forgive us, and he wants us to follow him so we can know him better each day. Knowing Jesus can change your life. And the more you know him, the better life will be.**

Pray: **Lord, we know that each of us has done wrong things. We thank you today for your forgiveness and for the new life you have for each of us. Thanks for wanting to know us individually. In Jesus' name, amen.**

18. The Greatest Gift of All
(1 Corinthians 13)

"Love" is perhaps the most abused word in the English language. We use it to describe how we feel about watching our favorite sport, petting the dog, or licking an ice cream cone. How ironic that the word we use to describe these common experiences is also the word we use to express the deepest of all human commitments: "I love you."

No wonder children are often confused about love. We can help them understand what God really means when he says, "Love one another." First Corinthians 13 describes real love as God intended it and helps us see how that kind of love can motivate everything we do in life. In this lesson, your students will explore this passage so they, too, can learn what love really is.

A POWERFUL POINT

Real love is the greatest gift we can give or receive.

A LOOK AT THE LESSON

1. Love Songs (6 minutes)
2. Reason Ruler (10 minutes)
3. Love Your Neighbor, Your Family, Your Friends... (8 minutes)
4. Heart Strings (15 minutes)
5. Gifts of Love (8 minutes)
6. Memories of Love (8 minutes)

THE FUN-TO-LEARN LESSON

1. Love Songs

(You'll need newsprint and markers.)

Form four teams. Give each team a sheet of newsprint and a marker. Say: **On "go," your team will have 60 seconds to think of as many songs with the word "love" in the title as you can. Write the titles on your newsprint. Ready? Go!**

When time is up, have teams tape their lists next to each other on the wall. Congratulate all the teams on their quick memories. Then ask:

● **Do you think all these songs tell the truth about love? Why or why not?**

● **If you wrote a song about love, what would you have it say?**

● **Why do you think people are often confused about what love really is?**

● **Do you know what love is? Explain.**

Say: **For many people, the definition of love is based on a song they hear or how they feel about someone they know. Doing that can be confusing because your feelings always change, and there are so many songs that say different things about what love really is. Fortunately, God has told us what love is supposed to be. Real love is the greatest gift we can give or** receive. **Today we're going to explore God's definition of love.**

2. Reason Ruler

(You'll need a marker, paper, masking tape, and Bibles.)

Using a bold marker, write the following reasons for doing things on separate sheets of paper: "Because I get paid," "Because I make someone happy when I do it," "Because someone will like me if I do it," "Because I show love when I do it," "Because someone will get mad if I don't do it," and "Because I love God."

Lay a strip of masking tape straight across the floor of the meeting room. At equal intervals along the masking tape, tape the papers on which you have written reasons for doing certain actions.

Say: **We've all been told that to love others you just have to treat people well and do nice things for them. But the love God talks about goes deeper than that. Real love must begin in the heart. Let's read about that deep love in 1 Corinthians 13:1-3.**

Read aloud 1 Corinthians 13:1-3. Then ask:

● **What do these verses say about doing nice things when "your heart's not in it"?**

● **Have you ever done something nice for someone, even though you didn't really want to? Explain.**

Say: **Sometimes our "kind acts" aren't really motivated by love. Let's see what really motivates us to do some of the nice things we do. I'm going to read a list of "nice" actions that we all probably do. After each action I read, decide why you usually do that activity and stand on the line next to that reason.**

Give kids 30 seconds to familiarize themselves with the reasons you've posted, then start the activity by reading the first action on the following list and allowing kids to move to a reason listed on the floor. Continue until kids have responded to all the actions on the following list. Here's the list:

● **Taking out the garbage**
● **Helping a friend with homework**
● **Walking the dog**
● **Buying someone a birthday present**
● **Cleaning up the kitchen**
● **Calling a friend on the phone**
● **Obeying your parent**
● **Spending recess with someone who looks lonely**

After the activity, have kids sit in trios. Tell trios to read 1 Corinthians 13:1-3 to each other with each person reading one verse. Ask:

● **What does this passage say about "why" we should do loving things?**

● **What did you discover about your "love" for others in this activity?**

● **What should you do when you don't "feel" like loving someone else from the heart?**

Say: **Real love is the greatest gift we can give or receive. But if we do loving things for others for all the wrong reasons, then that's not really love at all. We need to pray for God to change our hearts so we can love each other with the kind of real love described in 1 Corinthians 13.**

3. Love Your Neighbor, Your Family, Your Friends . . .

(You'll need newsprint, markers, and Bibles.)

Form groups of four. Tell groups to read aloud 1 Corinthians 13:4-13, with each group member reading two verses (one person will read just one verse). Say: **As you read this passage, think about ways you can show this kind of love to the people in your life.**

After they read the passage, have kids assign each of their group members one of these roles: car, train, plane, and boat. Send all the cars to one corner of the room, all the trains to another corner, all the planes to a third corner, and all the boats to the final corner.

Give each group one category of people with whom kids often interact; for example, family, people at school, people at church, and people in the community (such as the mail carrier, grocery store workers, or the local librarian). Also give each group a marker and a sheet of newsprint.

Say: **On your newsprint, list ways you can show real love to the group of people you've been assigned. Remember what you just read in 1 Corinthians 13 as you brainstorm ways to be loving. You'll have three minutes to think of as many ways to show love as you can.**

After three minutes, have kids return to their original groups and share with each other the ways they came up with for showing real love to people around them. Have each student choose one way to show love to someone in the coming week. Then have each one tell the person on the right one way that person already shows real love to others.

After kids share, gather everyone together and ask:

● **What are some of the acts of real love you came up with in your groups?**

● **Which acts of love did you decide to carry out in the coming week?**

● **Which qualities of love as described in 1 Corinthians 13 are you showing in each of these actions?**

Say: **God has given us all the capacity to love others with his kind of "real" love. But none of us is perfect at loving others the way we should. Let's look at how we can learn to love others better than we do now.**

4. Heart Strings

(You'll need wire hangers, red construction paper, scissors, string, hole punches, and Bibles.)

Say: **We're going to choose some "love qualities" from 1 Corinthians 13 that we want to get better at. Then we're going to build something fun to help us remember to work on those qualities in the coming weeks.**

Give each student a wire hanger, red construction paper, scissors, and string. Have one or more hole punches available.

Have students use the red construction paper to cut out five heart shapes. On each heart shape, have them write a different quality of love from 1 Corinthians 13 that they'd like to improve in themselves. Have students punch a hole near the top of each heart, then create a mobile using the string and the hanger (see diagram below).

When kids finish their mobiles, hang them from the ceiling or just have kids hold them up to explain the qualities of love they chose. Say: **Let's pray together that God will help us be loving in the ways we've selected. I'll start the prayer by reading the Bible passage aloud. When you hear a loving quality that you included on your mobile, stand up and then sit back down as a way of expressing your request to God. Let's pray.**

Pray: **Dear God, thank you for your great gift of real love that we can give and receive. Please help us love in the way you intended. Remind us that** (read 1 Corinthians 13:4-7 aloud here). **Thank you, God, that you love us with the most perfect love of all. In Jesus' name, amen.**

Say: **It's great to choose to love other people. Real love is the greatest gift you can give or receive. When we love others the way God loves us—from the heart—the love we give away actually blesses us, too. Now that we understand what God's love is all about, let's practice this love on each other.**

5. Gifts of Love

(You'll need wrapping paper, plain paper, pens, a basket, masking tape, and Bibles.)

Give each person a 6×6-inch square of wrapping paper, a slip of paper, and a pen. Have kids write their names on the slips of paper. Then put the names in a basket and have kids each pick out a name (not their own) from the basket. Make sure kids don't tell whose names they chose.

Say: **Think about all the qualities you like or admire about the person whose name you drew. On the** back of your wrapping paper, write at least one of those qualities for that person to read. For example, you might write, "I love the way you treat everyone the same" or "I like how you invite me to spend time with you." Pick qualities that in some way reflect the real love we've been talking about today.**

When kids finish, show them how to turn their paper square into a gift by folding all four corners until they touch together in the center (see diagram below). Distribute masking tape and have kids seal the corners of the gift with the tape, then write the person's name on the tape strip. Have kids exchange the gifts and read what others wrote for them.

Ask:
● **How does it feel to receive love from someone else in the room?**
● **How does it feel to give love?**

Say: **Use your gift this week as a reminder that God's real love is the greatest gift we can give or receive. Let your gift become a motivator for you as you plan your loving act for someone else in the coming days.**

6. Memories of Love

Form a circle and say: **Take a moment now to think about what we've done in this class today and what you've learned.**

After a moment or two, have kids

take turns telling one thing they've learned through this lesson that they'd like to share with others. For example, kids might say, "From making our mobiles, I learned it's important to grow in the qualities of love." Or kids might say, "From the activity with the masking tape on the floor, I learned that real love is the greatest gift we can give or receive."

When everyone has had an opportunity to share, have kids stand, form a huddle, and place their right hands in the center of the huddle. Dismiss by having everyone shout (football-huddle style), "Real love is the greatest gift we can give or receive!"

If you did the "Heart Strings" activity, encourage kids to take their mobiles home and hang them where kids will be frequently reminded to work on developing God's real love in their lives.

19. In God We Trust
(Hebrews 11)

Kids who grow up in loving homes learn to use "faith" all the time in their lives. They have faith that their parents will provide food for them to eat, faith that they'll have clothes to wear, even faith that their parents will love them no matter what. Unfortunately for many kids, this faith is shattered by broken promises and broken people who impact kids' lives. For these kids, having faith in God can seem uncertain at best and, at worst, impossible.

But having faith in God isn't like having faith in people, because God can never fail us. God has made many promises to us, and he will never let us down. In this lesson, students will discover the meaning of true faith in light of God's perfect love and faithfulness toward them.

A POWERFUL POINT

Faith means trusting God no matter what.

A LOOK AT THE LESSON

1. Of Course I'm Faithful (12 minutes)
2. Back-to-Back Faith (6 minutes)
3. Don't Pop My Trust (8 minutes)
4. The Faith Times (13 minutes)
5. Faithful Friends (7 minutes)
6. Cardly Faithful (7 minutes)
7. Circle of Faith (6 minutes)

THE FUN-TO-LEARN LESSON

1. Of Course I'm Faithful

(You'll need various classroom items such as a chair, a paper cup, and a table; a pitcher; a spoon; two bowls; and dry beans to create an obstacle course.)

Before class, create an obstacle course of things kids take for granted on a daily basis. Set up the room so kids will have to do things like:

● sit in a chair;

● pour water from a pitcher into a paper cup and drink it;

● crawl under a table; and

● take a spoonful of dry beans from one bowl and walk with it to another bowl and dump the beans.

When everyone has arrived, form two teams.

Say: **We're going to have a race to see which team can go through this obstacle course the fastest.**

Explain and demonstrate how the course works. Time each member of the first team as he or she runs the course in turn. Then repeat the process for the second team. The team that completes the course in the shortest time wins. After the race, ask:

● **Why weren't you afraid to sit in the chair? Why weren't you afraid to crawl under the table?**

● **What else did you have to trust in this obstacle course?**

● **Why wasn't it hard for you to trust these things?**

● **How would you define trust? faith?**

● **What kind of people do you trust? Explain.**

Say: **Faith is a word that means to have absolute trust in someone or something. We each demonstrate faith every day, often in ways we don't even realize. But faith in God is something we choose—it doesn't happen automatically. For Christians, faith means trusting God no matter what. Today we're going to talk about having faith in God. Let's start by doing an experiment in trust.**

2. Back-to-Back Faith

(You'll need Bibles.)

Have kids form pairs and sit back to back. Have one partner in each pair silently choose an object in the room that the other person can readily see. Tell the second person to determine what that object is by asking yes or no questions such as "Is it something I can hold in my hand?"

Once the guesser has guessed correctly, have the partners switch roles and play again. Afterward, ask:

● **How did you figure out what your partner's object was?**

● **What questions did you ask to figure it out?**

● **How did you know your partner was telling you the truth?**

● **How is having faith in your partner's truthfulness like having faith in God?**

● **How do we know we can safely believe in God?**

Have kids read aloud Hebrews 11:1 and 6 in unison. Then ask:

● **Based on these verses, what does it mean to have faith in God?**

● **Why is it important for us to have faith in God?**

● **How does having faith in God affect the way you live each day?**

Say: **Faith is trusting in God even though we can't see, hear, touch, smell, or taste him. Faith means trusting God no matter what. When we trust God in this way, we don't have to be afraid of the bad things that can happen to us in life.**

Ask:

● **What are some things you're afraid of in life?**

● **How can having faith in God help you not be afraid?**

Say: **God never promises to keep bad things from happening to us, but he does promise to take us safely through those painful times. When we trust in him, life doesn't seem so scary anymore.**

Let's take a deeper look into what it means to trust God no matter what.

3. Don't Pop My Trust

(You'll need balloons, markers, and string.)

Distribute balloons, string, and markers. Have kids inflate their balloons and tie them with a knot. Then instruct students to write their names on their balloons with a marker. Have students pair up and swap balloons with their partners. Give students each 2 feet of string and have them tie one end of the string to their partner's balloon and the other end to their own ankle.

Say: **We're going to play a game in which you try to pop as many balloons as you can. You will win the game if the balloon with your name on it is still unpopped when I call time. Remember that your partner has your balloon and you have** your partner's balloon. You have four minutes to pop as many balloons as possible. Ready? Go!

After four minutes, stop the game and congratulate all the kids whose partners kept their balloons safe.

Have pairs each find another pair to form foursomes. In their groups, have kids respond to three or four of the following questions.

Teacher Tip

If you have time, allow kids to discuss all nine of the questions in this activity. However, most groups will only be able to adequately discuss three to five of the questions included here—and that's OK. Give different groups different questions to discuss or simply choose the three questions you think are most compelling for your kids and have groups discuss those.

● **What was it like to trust someone else with your balloon?**

● **What was it like to have your partner trust you with his or her balloon?**

● **How is trusting your partner with your balloon like trusting God with your life?**

● **Why was it hard for some of us to trust our partners with our balloons?**

● **Why is it hard for people sometimes to trust God?**

● **Is it hard for you to trust God? Why or why not?**

● **What do you worry about most in life?**

● **What can you do this week to start trusting God more in that area of your life?**

Say: **Just like you trusted a partner to care for your balloon, you can trust God to care for the important things in your life. Faith means** trusting God no matter what. And the more faith we have, the easier it is for us to let him take care of our fears and worries.

Let's learn more about how we can strengthen our faith in God this week.

4. The Faith Times

(You'll need paper, pencils, and Bibles.)

Form four groups and distribute Bibles, paper, and pencils.

Say: **We're going to create a TV show called *Faith Times*. Your group will work as a team to write one scene for this TV show based on the Bible passages I'll assign to you.**

Assign the following passages:

● Group 1—Hebrews 11:4; Genesis 4:1-8 (Abel offers God a better sacrifice than Cain.)

● Group 2—Hebrews 11:7; Genesis 6:9–7:10; 7:17–8:1 (Noah builds the ark.)

● Group 3—Hebrews 11:17-19; Genesis 22:1-14 (Abraham offers Isaac as a sacrifice.)

● Group 4—Hebrews 11:29; Exodus 14:21-31 (Moses leads the Israelites across the Red Sea.)

Say: **As you read your passages, think about how you can create a TV scene that illustrates the faith you see demonstrated in the story. Then work together in your group to create a TV scene that you can act out for the rest of the class.**

Give the groups several minutes to read the passages and create their scenes. Be available to help kids with ideas for how to convert their Bible story into a TV skit. When everyone is done, have groups each present their TV scene.

Congratulate each group's creativity, then ask:

● **What sorts of worries and fears did the people in these stories face?**

● **How did they deal with their fears?**

● **What did God do for them in response to their faith?**

● **What do these stories tell us about having faith in God?**

● **How can these stories encourage you to trust God more deeply this week?**

Say: **The people in each of these stories understood that faith means trusting God no matter what. When we read their stories, we can see how God was faithful to them, and that can help us trust God with our worries and fears.**

5. Faithful Friends

(You'll need paper, pencils, and Bibles.)

Have kids return to their groups of four from the "Don't Pop My Trust" activity. Give everyone a Bible, a sheet of paper, and a pencil. Have kids take turns reading Hebrews 11:1-31 to their groups, with each person reading eight verses (one will read only seven verses).

When kids are finished reading, say: **We're going to write short faith stories about the people in our groups, just like the stories in Hebrews 11. Each of you will write a one- or two-sentence faith story about the person on your left. For example, you could write, "By faith, Morgan chooses to obey God by not taking illegal drugs or hanging around people who do."**

Encourage kids to ask the person on their left about any choices he or she has made recently based on faith in God. It could be something as sim-

ple as coming to church regularly or praying to God every day. When kids have finished writing their stories, have them share the stories within their groups.

Say: **Faith means trusting God no matter what. We can encourage each other to have faith in God by sharing our own faith stories and by noticing when someone else is trusting God—even in hard times. Now let's take a look at some specific ways God wants us to place our trust in him.**

6. Cardly Faithful

(You'll need playing cards and Bibles.)

Give each student two cards from a standard deck of cards.

Say: **We're going to play a bargaining game. Each of you has two cards. The object of this game is to get the highest total number with your two cards. All cards count for face value, jacks count for 11, queens count 12, and kings count 13.**

If you wish, you can trade cards with each other or bargain with each other in any way you want as long as you don't let anyone actually see your cards. For example, you can make a blind trade by picking (sight unseen) one of your friend's cards and having him or her pick one of yours. Or you can tell someone what cards you're holding and let them decide whether to believe you before taking one of your cards. You'll have three minutes to make your trades. Ready? Go!

Teacher Tip

If playing cards are inappropriate for your church or denomination, substitute 3×5 cards. You'll need to number the cards from 1 to 13 and create four cards for each number; for example, four "1" cards, four "2" cards, and so on.

After three minutes, call time and have kids total the numbers on their cards to determine who won. Ask:

● **How did you know who to trust when you made your trades, especially when you couldn't see their cards?**

● **How did it feel to trust someone and be let down?**

● **How did it feel to trust someone and find out they had told you the truth?**

Have a volunteer read aloud Hebrews 11:13-16. Ask:

● **How was trusting each other in this game like or unlike trusting God in real life?**

● **How can we know God isn't lying to us when he says he loves us and will take care of us?**

● **Do you believe God loves you and will take care of you? Why or why not?**

● **What other things does God promise us?**

● **What does it mean for you to have faith in God no matter what?**

Say: **Sometimes people in this world make empty promises. They tell you one thing but do another.**

But God *always* keeps his promises. We can have faith in him no matter what happens in our lives.

7. Circle of Faith

Say: **We've been learning about having faith in God. Now let's bring that lesson down to a more personal level.**

Have kids each select an object in the room that represents a way they need God to help them in their lives. For example, a pencil could mean that someone needs God to help him or her at school. When kids have each found an object, have them sit in a circle on the floor and place the objects in the center of the circle.

When all the kids are seated, go around the circle and have kids share what their objects represent.

Then say: **We all need to deepen our faith in God. Each object represents just one way we need to learn to have faith in God no matter what. To help us believe, let's pray together for God's help.**

Have kids join hands in the circle, then pray aloud: **Dear God, we give you these objects in the center of our circle. They represent the parts of our lives that we want to trust you with. We believe in your love for us and in your commitment to care for our needs. Please help us trust you with these things. Please be faithful to care for them. Thank you, amen.**

20. Good Heaven!
(The New Heaven and New Earth)

Kids love to receive things that are brand new. They can go crazy over a new pair of jeans, a new book, a new anything—especially when the new item replaces something that's worn out.

Imagine how they'll feel when God creates a new heaven and a new earth! Use this lesson to help kids celebrate God's promise of a new heaven and a new earth.

A POWERFUL POINT

God has promised us a new heaven and a new earth.

A LOOK AT THE LESSON

1. God Cannot Be Crushed (5 minutes)
2. New and Improved (8 minutes)
3. Rotating Discussion (7 minutes)
4. Movin' On and Up! (12 minutes)
5. Foil Prayers (6 minutes)
6. Affirmation Wall (8 minutes)
7. Heavenly Singing (7 minutes)

THE FUN-TO-LEARN LESSON

1. God Cannot Be Crushed

(You'll need paper.)

Have students form trios and give each trio a sheet of paper.

Say: **We're going to try our hands at changing something old into something new. Each trio has a piece of brand new paper. I want you to take your piece of paper and crumple it into the tightest ball you can, like this.**

Demonstrate crumpling a piece of paper into a tight ball, then allow time for trios to copy your actions. Next say: **Now, you have one minute to try to make your piece of paper look like new again. Use whatever method you think will do the trick (except for getting a new piece of paper). Ready? Go!**

After one minute, compare each trio's paper with a fresh piece of paper. Then ask:

● **What do you think it would take to make this old sheet of paper new again?**

● **What are some things in our world that you wish could be made new again?**

● **What would it take for us to make them new again?**

Say: **There are a lot of things in our world that are broken and need fixing. For example, pollution hurts our environment, and violence hurts people who live in our cities. Even our families are often broken, and we wish we could make them new, too. Sometimes we can fix things to make them new again, but most times we can't. But God can fix anything, and today we're going to learn about how he promises to make for us a new heaven and a new earth.**

2. New and Improved

Form three groups. Say: **We've all seen commercials for products that claim to be "new and improved." What if we were to create a "new and improved" world? What would it look like? Here's your opportunity to create a commercial for a new earth. Each group will make up a commercial, and then we'll share our commercials with each other.**

Give the groups three minutes to develop their commercials. Then have each group perform its commercial for the other two groups. Ask:

● **What would it be like if we could really make our new and improved worlds a reality?**

● **What keeps us from making our world new and improved?**

Have a volunteer read aloud Romans 8:19-21. Then ask:

● **According to this passage, why hasn't God already made a new heaven and a new earth?**

Say: **God promises that he will make a new heaven and a new earth when the time is right. In our next activity we're going to look at how God will do this.**

3. Rotating Discussion

(You'll need Bibles.)

Form two circles, one inside the other. Have the inside circle face outward and the outside circle face inward. Have kids pair up with the person facing them, so each person has a partner from the other circle. Give kids each a Bible.

Say: **The person in front of you is now your partner. I'll ask you a question to discuss with him or her. Then you'll share your answers with the rest of the class. When we're done with the first question, everyone in the inside circle will rotate one position to the left. I'll ask another question, and you'll repeat the process with your new partner.**

(If you have six or fewer kids in your class, make two lines facing each other. For each new question have the kids in one line move to the left. Have the person on the left end of the line move to the right end of the line during the rotation.)

Ask:

● **Read Revelation 21:1-7. What does God say about the new heaven and the new earth?**

After a minute, get the group's attention, and have pairs share their answers to the question. Then have the inside circle rotate to the left, and ask another question. Repeat the process until the kids have answered all of the following questions:

● **Revelation 21:3 says God will live with us on earth. What do you think that will be like?**

● **According to Revelation 21:1-7, what will be different about the new earth than earth as we know it today?**

● **How does knowing that God will create a new heaven and a new earth affect how you think about the world now? the way you feel about the people you see every day?**

● **How will you share what you learn today with somebody else this week?**

Say: **Because God promises us a new heaven and a new earth, we have something wonderful to look forward to. It gives us hope when life in this present world gets hard.**

Let's take a closer look at how life will change for us when we reach God's new heaven.

4. Movin' On and Up!

(You'll need a suitcase, a wastebasket, paper, markers, and Bibles.)

Place an open suitcase and a wastebasket in the front of the room. Form trios. Have trios designate one person as the reader, one as the writer, and one as the speaker. Give each trio two sheets of paper and a marker.

Say: **When we think about being with God in heaven, it's like looking forward to moving to a brand new house. When we move to a new house, we pack our suitcases with the things we plan to take with us. We also throw away the things we don't need anymore. I have a suitcase and a wastebasket up here. We're going to pack what God says we'll take with us to heaven, and we're going to throw away what God says we won't need anymore.**

Have the readers read Revelation 21:1-7 to their groups.

When they're finished reading, say: **Think of one thing from this world that will not be a part of the new heaven or new earth. For example, crying will not be a part of the new heaven or new earth. Once you think of your item, have your writer draw a picture or write a sentence that represents your group's answer. For example, for crying you could draw tears.**

Then think of something that *will* be a part of the new heaven and new earth; for example, friendship. On your other sheet of paper, draw a picture or write a sentence that represents this answer. For example, for friendship you could write, "My friends will be with me in heaven." Continue until you have listed at least five items on each sheet of paper.

When trios are done with their drawings or sentences, say: **Let's pack our things for moving to the new heaven and new earth.**

Have the speakers from each trio bring their trio's drawings to the front of the room. Have them each tell what they would throw away, then toss their "throw away" sheet into the wastebasket. Then have speakers each tell what they would pack to take with them and put that picture or sentence into the suitcase.

Once all the groups have shared, review the items that kids tossed into the wastebasket and packed into the suitcase. Then ask:

● **What's your reaction to knowing that all the items tossed into the wastebasket will someday be destroyed forever?**

● **What thoughts come to mind when you consider all the items we've packed in our suitcase?**

● **How can knowing about these things change the way you think about life right now?**

Say: **We have so much to look forward to because of God's promise of a new heaven and a new earth. When we get there, we won't experience things that make us sad anymore, and everything will be new. In the meantime, we can focus our attention on the things we know will go with us when we enter the new heaven and the new earth.**

Have kids each turn to a partner and respond to these questions:

● **What's one item in this suitcase that you especially value in your life today?**

● **What's one thing you can do this week to focus more of your attention on that item?**

● **What's one quality you see in your partner that reminds you of heaven? For example, it could be** your partner's smile or the way you value your friendship with him or her.

Say: **We can always find hints of the new heaven and new earth in the people around us. And that can prompt us to thank God for the wonderful new heaven and new earth that are still to come. Let's do that now.**

5. Foil Prayers

(You'll need aluminum foil and permanent markers.)

Give each student a piece of foil and a marker.

Say: **On your piece of foil, write a prayer thanking God for one thing you're looking forward to in the new heaven and new earth. For example, you could write, "Thank you, God, for your promise of a new heaven and a new earth. I thank you that someday I won't have to feel sad about my parents' divorce. Amen."**

Give students time to write out their prayers.

Say: **Let's pray about what we just wrote. I'll start, then I'll give you a moment to silently pray what you just wrote.**

Pray: **Dear God, we look forward to the new heaven and new earth that you'll create someday. Knowing that you'll do this gives us hope for today.**

Say: **Now silently pray your foil prayer.**

Give kids a minute to pray.

Pray aloud: **Thank you, God, for your promise of a new heaven and a new earth. Amen.**

Encourage kids to carefully fold their foil prayers and take them home as a reminder of this lesson.

6. Affirmation Wall

(You'll need red construction paper, transparent tape, and markers.)

Before the meeting, cut red construction paper into 4×9-inch rectangles and tape them to the wall in the form of a brick wall (see diagram below). Don't write anything in the bricks yet. Make enough bricks so every student can have at least one.

Assemble kids in front of the brick wall you prepared before class. Say: **God is beginning a new heaven and a new earth in us right now. Let's think of words to describe how he's doing that; for example: kindness.** (Write "kindness" on one of the bricks.) **Kindness is one way in which God is creating a new heaven and a new earth in us today. What are some other ways?**

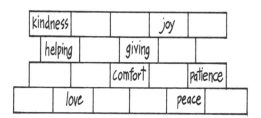

Have kids volunteer more words. Write one word per brick. Encourage the kids to think of as many words as there are bricks.

When you've written on every brick, have each person pick a brick off the wall and hand it to someone to whom they feel that word applies. When they do this, have them share why they feel that word describes the person they gave it to. For example, someone might choose a brick that says "gentleness" and say that the recipient is always gentle when someone is sad.

Continue this process until everyone has received a brick and given a brick to someone else.

Say: **One day God will create a totally new heaven and new earth. But when we tell others how much we appreciate them, we can see that God has already begun his work by creating a new heaven and a new earth for us in our hearts. We can rejoice in what God is creating in us right now because it's like a "piece" of the new heaven and earth to come.**

7. Heavenly Singing

(You'll need hymnals.)

Form three groups. Give each group a hymnal and the page number of a hymn about heaven. Use "heaven" songs that are familiar to your students.

Say: **We're going to close our** time together by singing about heaven. Each group will sing a song for the other two groups. I've told you which song you'll sing, but before you sing your hymn, you must create a new tune for it. For example, you could sing your song to the tune of another familiar song, such as "Mary Had a Little Lamb" or the *Gilligan's Island* theme song or any other tune you like.

Give the groups two minutes to decide on a tune and to rehearse. Then have the groups sing their songs for each other.

After the songs, say: **Remember these songs this week and thank God that he has promised us a new heaven and a new earth.**